Rita F. Snowden is wide... the author of more than s... ...books for adults and children. After six years at business she trained as a deaconess of the New Zealand Methodist Church, serving in turn two pioneer country areas before moving to the largest city for several years of social work during an economic depression.

Miss Snowden has served the world Church, beyond her own denomination, with regular broadcasting commitments. She has written and spoken in Britain, Canada, the United States, in Australia, and in Tonga at the invitation of Queen Salote. She has represented her church at the World Methodist Conference in Oxford; later being elected the first woman Vice-President of the New Zealand Methodist Church, and President of its Deaconess Association. She has been an Honorary Vice-President of the New Zealand Women Writers' Society, and is a Fellow of the International Institute of Art and Letters, and a member of P.E.N.

Miss Snowden has been honoured by the award of the Order of the British Empire, and by the citation of "The Upper Room" in America.

Her most recent books are *Prayers for Busy People, Christianity Close to Life, Bedtime Stories and Prayers* (for children), *I Believe Here and Now, Discoveries That Delight, Further Good News, Continually Aware, Good Company, Prayers in Large Print, Like Wind on the Grasses* and *Secrets*.

Rita Snowden

PEOPLE AND PLACES

Collins
FOUNT PAPERBACKS

First published in 1987
by Fount Paperbacks, London

Copyright © Rita F. Snowden 1987

Made and printed in Great Britain by
William Collins Sons & Co. Ltd, Glasgow

Unless otherwise stated, all Bible quotations
are taken from the Authorized Version
of the Bible.

Dedicated
to Dr Pauline Webb,
blessed with a wide knowledge
of people and places

Contents

Introduction

I clearly remember the title of the first book I ever wrote, *Through Open Windows*, but not, I must confess, the title of the first book I ever read, a long time earlier. It seems that it was a little book of stories – but it hasn't survived. Nor have a number of others eagerly, innocently lent to friends. That was before I provided my book-loving self with a series of little notebooks. Sir Walter Scott used to say of his friends that he wasn't sure whether they were good at arithmetic – but he knew that some of them were good "book-keepers".

For years now, I haven't lost a book, but I pick the moment carefully when I see a friend scanning my shelves, and lifting out one of my favourites. Then I say softly: "I know you won't mind my taking a note of it; you see, these are 'my friends', or 'my tools' [according to the nature of the book, and of the 'book-keeper'] and I might just want it in a hurry!"

And this simple scheme works. People are impressed by the fact that I know where my property is – and, of course, I do. If a book is not forthcoming after what I count a reasonable time, I find I can always now recover it, without loss of good relationships. But it's essential to resort to that little notebook before my friend goes off with my book, so that he knows, and I know – and he knows that I know – where it is! A fellow book lover, lender, and writer, Philip Gibbs, was once heard to say: "It's better to give than to lend – and it costs about the same." It's plain he hadn't a little notebook handy. For so often it happens, when good talk of good books develops among enthusiasts, that one will be heard to say sadly: "I used to have that on my shelves, but somebody seems to have forgotten to return it."

Yet I have to say that a borrowed book lacks something of the joy of a book possessed.

*   *   *

It so happens that the little book I want to write about now, as a treasure, is one I've never been asked to lend: Mark's little book, the very first Christian gospel in the world! Matthew, Mark and Luke, the three of them, share one title: "The Synoptic Gospels", the word, in Greek, meaning *to see together*.

But each has something special to contribute, and the one I want to share has brief, graphic word pictures that are quite unforgettable.

Papias (Bishop of Hierapolis in the second century) was a great collector of gospel facts, and he confirmed that young Mark's book was made up, for the most part, from the preaching material of Peter. (If you revel in figures in a way I cannot claim to do, you might be fascinated to know from scholars with a like passion, that whereas Mark's gospel comes to us in 661 verses, Matthew chose to "lift" 606 of them, and Luke 320, *such was the debt they owed to Mark!*)

You may not have heard of Thomas Jefferson's efforts to write a book called *An Abridged New Testament for the Indians – unembarrassed by matters of fact and faith beyond their comprehension*. It was made up, he claimed, "of the earthly life story and ethical teaching of Jesus, as a good man – *with all the divine factors left out*". But Mark's book, for all that it was so small, was never like that. Such a compilation cannot rightly be called "a gospel". In Mark's presentation, the redeeming power of Jesus is plain to all. His gospel is a great deal more than a hero-story; it has a glorious balance, telling of things human and Divine. And that makes it a treasurable possession!

The little book actually begins, as you must have noticed, with the striking words: "*The Gospel of Jesus Christ, the Son of God*" (Mark 1:1). And throughout, there is no missing the awe Jesus evoked in young Mark's mind and spirit. Not only has his book a steady reverence, but it reaches out with a breathtaking eagerness and immediacy. This shows up at once, in his early use of the word translated for us as *straightway* (1:10): "And *straightway* coming up out of the water [at His baptism by John the Baptist, in the river Jordan] He saw the heavens opened, and the Spirit like a dove descending upon Him: and there came a voice from heaven, saying: '*Thou art My beloved Son, in Whom I am well pleased!*' " And before this first chapter is ended, Mark has used this word, as well as a companion word, "immediately", each four times, and he goes on using them throughout the whole of his writing. They are a young man's words, spelling out swift action!

By the time he reaches the end of his first vital chapter, Jesus, of course, is no longer alone for He has chosen His first disciples: "and *straightway*", we read, "they forsook their nets and followed Him" (18).

It must, I think, have been much harder for them to acknowledge Him as both human and Divine than it is for us, since from childhood they had been taught that God was *one God*; and regularly, with the opening of each Jewish gathering for worship, a voice was raised in declaration of it. Yet here was Jesus, following on the dramatic experience of His baptism, *claiming Oneness with God!* – something which was to be later confirmed by God, on the Mount of Transfiguration (Mark 9:2). There, after a shining experience, "a cloud overshadowed them; and a voice came out of the cloud, saying, 'This is My beloved Son: *hear Him!*' "

Side by side the disciples, talking, travelling, eating, sleeping, through days and nights, found the two sides of

His personality, human and Divine, accepted as one. (If there had been any lack of manliness, those strong fishermen, their regular nightly toil filled with hazard, wouldn't have owned Him "Master!" as they did.)

And as time passed, in glad company and in solitariness, and often amidst milling, demanding crowds, they saw no evidence that the Holiness of God ever rebuked Him. Even when, much later, He hung between earth and heaven on the infamous Hill of Crosses Three, the words of a hard-living Roman soldier involved in that dastardly deed, were such that Peter would never forget: "*Truly, this man was the Son of God!*"

Much of what Mark wrote into his gospel, opening with the words: "The beginning of the Gospel of Jesus Christ, the Son of God", comes to us, as Dr William Barclay loved to say, "with the freshness and closeness of someone who was there." And that, of course, was how it was. Mark's good home afforded some experience, but his close friend, Peter, was present again and again when Jesus was teaching, preaching, and healing. Thus it was that Mark was able to pick up some very personal stories.

Only Mark tells how Jesus, after a demanding time ministering "to the multitude", "fell asleep on a pillow" in "the hinder part of the ship", when His fishermen friends had whisked Him away. And "a great storm" got up – and still He slept, till fearful (despite all their shared experience of ships and storms), they wakened Him with the abrupt words: "Master, carest Thou not that we perish?" – words charged with alarm! And He arose, and immediately took charge of the situation! In Mark's record it comes to us in such detail. What a graphic word picture of the costliness of that ministry to the multitudes! (Mark 4:35–41).

He tells in his gospel how the Master, one day in His teaching, gently centred attention upon a child – and more than that, took him up in His arms! (Mark 9:36–37).

And only Mark tells of the young man who came

"running" to Jesus in a public place, so eagerly, but then found that he couldn't face the challenge put to him, and "went away sorrowful". And Jesus, "looking upon him, loved him!" (Mark 10:17–22).

On an earlier occasion, Mark finds space in his little book for another very personal "moment". The Master is dealing on this occasion, not with one young man, but with a little girl, and on the way to her, with an old woman – all so personal!

Coming So Freshly

So eager was Mark to pass on to his readers, without loss, what had come to him that again and again he slipped into his telling original Aramaic words. Many of them still remain to this day, in our cherished Authorized Version. This must strike any thoughtful reader when, in a day like ours, so many Bible versions are available.

In Mark's little gospel, as it has come down to us, so freshly, we meet throughout a sprinkling of these words, known every one of them to his earliest readers. The first Aramaic word here concerns Jesus' ministry.

It has to do with an anxious family who had a sick little daughter. "One of the rulers of the synagogue," we read, "Jairus by name, fell at His feet, and besought Him greatly, saying, 'My little daughter lieth at the point of death: I pray Thee, come and lay Thy hands on her, that she may be healed . . .' " And Mark says, "Jesus went with him; and much people followed . . . " (Mark 5:22-24). To the poor father, Jairus, haste must have seemed the essence of the undertaking, but no sooner had they started on their way, than they were interrupted. It was nothing new; this time it was a poor woman with a longtime distress of a very humiliating type. And she had by now been to numerous physicians, none of whom had been able to relieve her of an issue of blood – a haemorrhage, to use our unwelcome word – from which she had suffered for twelve years. In at least two of the modern versions of Mark's little book that I have, "The Moffatt Translation" and "The New English Bible", that grim word itself appears. "When she had heard of Jesus, she came in the press behind," I read, "and she touched His garment. For she said, 'If I may but touch

His clothes, I shall be whole.' " *What faith – after all those years, all those physicians, all those hopes continually revived only to be dashed!*

But she was rewarded "*straightway*" – and here is an unquestioned occasion when the beauty of that word shines out, a word of immediacy, of responsibility, when there's no time to waste. The translator of the New Testament tells us, from Mark: "the fountain of her blood was dried up; and she felt in her body that she was healed of that plague. Knowing in Himself", Mark says of Jesus, "that virtue had gone out of Him, He turned Him about in the press, and said, 'Who touched My clothes?' And His disciples said unto Him, 'Thou seest the multitude thronging Thee, and sayest Thou, "Who touched Me?" ' " ("Have a little sense!" in modern-day speech. "Whoever dared ask such a thing?")

So Mark says, "He looked round to see her that had done this thing. But the woman fearing and trembling, knowing what was done in her, came and fell down before Him, and told all the truth. And He said unto her, 'Daughter, thy faith hath made thee whole; go in peace, and be whole of thy plague' " (Mark 5:25-34). Wonderful!

But how long did it take? Was not Jairus already more than anxious? What about his own little daughter? "Why couldn't this woman have waited? What did she want to push in for?"

And Mark catches the anxiety of it, the speed of it, as he sets about recording it. "While He yet spake," he adds, recording the mood of things, "there came from the ruler of the synagogue's house, certain which said, 'Thy daughter is dead: why trouble thou the Master any further?' [Poor man! If it hadn't been for that woman, they'd have been there in time. Oh, dear! – but Mark didn't put that in!] As soon as Jesus heard the word that was spoken, He saith unto the ruler of the synagogue (Jairus) 'Be not afraid, only believe.' " What a wonderful

16

word of support that was, in that moment of family desperation!

So they came to the home of Jairus and his family, and made their way in. "And He suffered no man to follow Him," we read, "save Peter, and James, and John the brother of James." And then there is mention of "the tumult, and them that wept and wailed greatly". "These", says a scholar nearer our own time, "may well have been professional mourners – them that chanted the funeral dirge."

Throughout most of the ancient world in those times – in Palestine, Roman areas, Greece, Phoenicia and Assyria – it was the done thing to engage professional flute-players, together with wailing instruments and screeching voices, on an occasion of death or tragedy. It was counted essential. However poor a man might be, he should have at least two flute-players at a family funeral.

Added to them would always be the screams of neighbours who soon gathered to rend their garments and tear their hair, making passionate appeals to the dead. On this occasion, the ruler of the synagogue would be a man of some affluence, able to engage a maximum number of professional mourners. No wonder we read of Jesus: "And when He was come in, He saith unto them, 'Why make ye this ado, and weep? The damsel is not dead, but sleepeth.' *And they laughed Him to scorn*" (Mark 5:40).

"But when He had put them all out, He taketh the father and the mother of the damsel, and them that were with Him, and entereth in where the damsel was lying. And He took the damsel by the hand, and saith unto her, *Talitha cumi*!" [Aramaic words for the freshness and reality of his report, Mark felt he could not part with them – and I put them in here because, again and again through his gospel, Mark uses an Aramaic word for the same reason. And it's good that we should be on the lookout for them, as we enter into Mark's little book. We have them still in our long-loved Authorized Version and, perhaps more surprisingly, in many of our modern translations: *Talitha koum*, which is "Damsel, I say unto thee, arise", as the Good News Bible has it: " Little girl, I tell you to get up!"]

"*And straightway*" we go on – using that lively word again – "the damsel arose, and walked; for she was of the age of twelve years. And they were astonished with a great astonishment. And He charged them straightly that no man should know it; and *commanded that something should be given her to eat.*" (That's a nice, understanding touch, isn't it, saying much for the Master's carefulness; and for Mark's love of detail, that he recorded it!)

And so ends gloriously what must for long have seemed a family disaster, surrounded by distressing noise, and contrasting unforgettably with the calm, quiet capacity of Jesus, the Master and Lord of Life!

*　　*　　*

And it would be a loss to miss elsewhere in Mark's gospel another Aramaic word that fell very meaningfully from the lips of Jesus in 7:3. (To get it in its setting, it is helpful to start a few verses before the word actually appears, (32)) "They bring unto Him one that was deaf, and had an impediment in his speech; and they beseech Him to put His hands upon him." (To this day, as doubtless you have observed, these two troubles seem to go together, deafness and dumbness.) Jesus, with His customary handling of such a situation, "took the man aside from the multitude" and dealt with him. "And looking up to heaven, sighed, and saith unto him, *Ephphatha*!" (An Aramaic word that served very suitably, in the situation in which they found themselves, "*Be opened*!") "And *straightway* [typical word again, in response] his ears were opened, and the string of his tongue was loosed, and he spake plain."

And even when "earth-time" was running out for Jesus,

we find Mark recording another brief, beautiful Aramaic word, commonly on the lips of the Master, and yet another from the Cross – but we must wait to consider those, in their proper setting, at the proper time.

Sharing Life

Early "followers" of the Master caught, in time, something of the zeal of Mark's colleagues – and pressed on to share the Faith. For some time, by then, there had been men and women who had seen and heard the historical Jesus – and others who had opened their homes, as did Aquila and Priscilla. This couple was widely known and loved, being mentioned in the Book of Acts, carrying the early story of the Christian Church in the world (Acts 18:1; Moffatt). "After this Paul left Athens and went to Corinth. There he came across a Jew called Aquila, a native of Pontus, who had recently arrived from Italy with his wife Priscilla, as Claudius had ordered all Jews to leave Rome." Paul accepted them, as they belonged to the same trade, and he stayed with them as they worked together – making tents. And they shared also the risks faced by the "Church" at that time. Night by night, they opened their home, as was the custom in those early times before special buildings were raised for "Christian" worship. And those who did that ran many risks – men and women who, darting from the shadow of one back-street to the next, made their way to worship.

When Paul could no longer be of their company, he wrote letters to them, when a chance turned up that somebody trustworthy was going that way, and could carry them. (It is hard for us to think how life was in a world where there was no postal service, no newspapers, no "Christian" books, and where it was so dangerous to assemble for worship. For most it was a lonely experience. But Paul was not one to forget them; and his letters are treasured now in our New Testament, as when in Romans

16:3 (Moffatt) he was moved to write: "Salute Prisca [Priscilla] and Aquila, my fellow workers in Christ Jesus, who have *risked their lives for me.*"

In time Dr Luke, writing his book (Acts 15:26; Moffatt), used that same chilling word "risk". He there spoke of Paul and Barnabas "who have risked their lives for the sake of our Lord Jesus Christ." Barnabas was Mark's cousin, so Mark early knew what was involved in their way of life. For his own mother, Mary in Jerusalem, was one who opened her own door to such "travellers".

She was a leading figure, her affluence and generous hospitality widely, though secretly, known. Peter, Mark's close friend, was only one of a number who stayed there, in the city, when on his hazardous journeys. (And it was there, it seems certain to us now, that Mark came to know that valiant spirit, and as the years passed, became his friend. We have little doubt that it was to Mark's mother's welcoming home, that Peter made his way on the occasion when he managed to escape from prison. What, in such a crisis, more natural than to turn his hurrying steps in that direction?) For "King Herod", we read (Acts 12:1; Moffatt), "laid hands of violence on some members of the Church. James the brother of John he slew with the sword, and when he saw this pleased the Jews, he went on to seize Peter . . . After arresting him, he put him in prison, handing him over to a guard of sixteen soldiers, with the intention of producing him to the people after the Passover.

"So Peter was closely guarded in prison, while earnest prayer for him was offered to God by the Church." (That gives a graphic picture of all involved in these risks – and Mark would hear the talk that went on; and perhaps be present when others prayed for his friend Peter.) Dr Luke's record of Acts 12:6, in Moffatt's rendering, goes on to say graphically: "The very night before Herod meant to have him produced, Peter lay asleep between two soldiers;

he was fastened by two chains, and sentries in front of the door guarded the prison. But an angel of the Lord flashed on him, and a light shone in the cell; striking Peter on the side he woke him, saying, 'Quick, get up!' The fetters dropped from his hands, and the angel said to him, 'Gird yourself and put on your sandals.' He did so. Then said the angel, 'Put on your coat and follow me.' And he followed him out, not realizing that what the angel did was real, but imagining that he saw a vision. When they had passed the first guard and the second, they came to the iron gate leading into the city, which opened to them of its own accord; they passed out, and after they had gone through one street, the angel immediately left him. Then Peter came to his senses, and said, 'Now I know for certain that the Lord has sent His angel and rescued me from the hands of Herod and from all that the Jewish people were anticipating.'

"When he grasped the situation, he went to the house of Mary, the mother of John who was surnamed Mark, where a number had met for prayer." Then follows the nice little domestic story of the housemaid, Rhoda, answering a knock at the door of the porch. But "as soon as she recognized Peter's voice, instead of opening the door she ran inside from sheer joy and announced that Peter was standing in front of the porch. 'You are mad', they said. But she insisted it was true."

And, of course it was! (Read the record through, and let the drama of it hold you, remembering all the time that it was Mark's mother, Mary's, home.) But it was not all over yet. Verse 18 says: "When the day broke there was a great commotion among the soldiers over what had become of Peter. Herod made inquiries for him, but could not find him, so, after cross-examining the guards, he ordered them all to death." Poor fellows! It was not their fault – Herod was up against something that he didn't understand.

*   *   *

That time – above all others – Peter must have been glad of the hospitality of Mark's mother's home. There are numerous dependable scholars harking back to good Bishop Papias, who express gratitude for Peter's valuable help with the writing of Mark's Gospel.

* * *

And now we have another possibility, accepted by many dependable Christian scholars, which is that it was in an upper room in this same hospitable home in Jerusalem that Jesus's disciples, under His direction, prepared "the Last Supper". (It sounds, the more one thinks of it, natural enough.) "This", wrote my friend, Dr William Barclay, "may well be the explanation of two very odd verses in Mark" (Mark 14:51,52).

The Supper had come to its end, and the company had, with a hymn, gone out into the night. "And there followed Him", we read, "a certain young man, having a linen cloth cast about his naked body; and the young men laid hold of him; and he left the linen cloth and fled from them naked!" "Why", asks Dr Barclay, "is that strange, seemingly irrelevant verse, put into the Gospel?"

"Maybe", he answers, "because the young man was Mark himself, in whose home the Supper had been shared and who had fled out into the night. This could have been Mark's 'signature' on his Gospel."

Speaking for many beside myself – and certainly for myself – I am eager to know all I reasonably can about the writer of this little book, and about its message. Did young Mark, on that unforgettable night, listening closely from his own nearby room, hear the Supper company stir and – feeling that he couldn't bear to have Jesus go out into the unfriendly dark, with the possibility of desperate happenings – dash after Him? We don't know and never can know for sure. But the Master's place of retirement for prayer in Gethsemane was plainly no secret.

Yet there are things we can know for sure about the writer of this lively little book. Mark was undoubtedly close to members of the Christian fellowship, both men and women, including Peter, who called at his home when his journeys afforded that opportunity. More than that, Mark was born a kinsman of Barnabas, he was not just an admirer. And when Paul and Barnabas were planning to set out together on a certain missionary journey, it seemed to everyone involved a splendid idea to take young Mark with them: it would be a good adventure for him; and he would be able to show himself useful.

But when they got away together – somehow it didn't work out. By the time they got to Perga, the whole plan fell apart (Acts 13:13). Recording it later, Dr Luke could only say: "Now when Paul and his company loosed from Paphos, they came to Perga in Pamphylia: John Mark" – using his full family name – "departing from them, returned to Jerusalem." He'd had enough.

And why was that? Was the going too hard for a young fellow, a city boy, day after day? We do know that at this time Paul eagerly wanted to strike inland, to go up to the central plateau, and that for some unstated reason Mark didn't welcome the idea. Did he feel that this was far enough? Was he homesick? Was it that gradually the leadership of the little company was being assumed by Paul, and that Mark's special loyalty was towards his cousin, Barnabas? Or was it careless talk of brigands? We can never know.

In time, having finished their first missionary journey one man short, they proposed to set out again. (And Barnabas was still keen to take Mark.) But Paul refused to have anything to do with such a plan (Acts 15:37), as the record makes plain. "Barnabas determined to take with them", the A.V. says, "John, whose surname was Mark." (But Paul's memories of their experience at Perga stood in the way of that. And he wouldn't be moved – nor would cousin Barnabas, for that matter.) "And the contention was so sharp between them," verse 39 goes on to say, "that they departed asunder, one from the other; and so Barnabas took Mark, and sailed unto Cyprus."

*   *   *

Somewhere – we are not sure just where or when – Mark began his graphic little book. But it was written, that is certain, out of a loving heart and an awareness of Jesus amongst men and women. How amazed he would be, could he know in how many millions of copies, and in how many lands, (like my own – not even discovered on the face of the earth, in his lifetime) it would appear, and that there would be countless readers to this day, you and I among them!

Two reasons why this first of the gospels was so long in coming, was that the cost of producing a properly scribed book was, in those simple times, so very high. A book was measured out in stichois, a stichos being, scholars tell us, about the length of an average hexametre line of poetry from Homer, the great epic poet of Greece. Later, the Roman Emperor fixed the price of most things, and by that edict, the pay of a good scribe was 20-25 denarii per hundred stichois. And from another source, we learn that even in Mark's little book, there were about 1600 stichois. A denarius, at the time the prices were fixed, was about nine pence – so you can work out, if this kind of thing interests you, how much you would have needed in your hand to buy even so small a book, remembering that you would have had to take into account the changing purchasing power of the coinage. Therefore, to buy a book was one of the last things that Christians thought to do.

And even today, in some places this is still a grievous admission, although generally things are very different. There are Christians who, seemingly, never think of their privilege of living in a "book age" – and the odd one here and there who doesn't even know how to go about acquiring a book.

When the war came, and I had to cease travelling all over the country with books – both because the Japanese threatened and petrol was limited – I came back to service in the city Epworth Bookroom. As the next few years went by, I learnt some more about "book-buyers".

One day a woman came in, looking a little bewildered, and without so much as a greeting asked whether she could buy a Bible. My first natural question was: "What sort of Bible?" – meaning, did she want one with a handsome binding and fine India paper, or one in a cloth cover, fit for a child to carry to Sunday School? This only confused her further. "All I know", she said, "is that I'm to get the one with the Methodist words in it." I understood from that that her children had just started at a Methodist Sunday School, and she wanted to be sure to get the book they used! When I reported it to the rest of the staff at teatime we laughed – but it wasn't really a laughing matter.

Mark's little gospel – within the New Testament, within the Bible sought, has never been the sole possession of "the Methodists". Indeed, there were no such Christians when Mark's vivid gospel, leading the others, set out into the world!

* * *

A further reason why some early Christians felt it hardly worth the work, and cost, to put their Risen Lord and Master's earth-story into a book, was that they took His words literally, and when He spoke about His "coming again", expected it to be any day soon, so they felt it hardly worth the toil of "gospel making". They were, in any case, so accustomed to having truth passed on to them by *the spoken word*!

Close and Real

But I am eager to share unexpected things that have happened to people in our day, through having come across Mark's little gospel! (It is, of course, wonderful to have all four gospels bound up beautifully together in the New Testament, but we're thinking just now of the one Mark gave to us – the first, and the shortest!) Around us now, in fine bookshops in great cities, and in theological college libraries, are countless learned tomes on it – but lives are more than "tomes"!

I would like to introduce Anthony Bloom – though you may have already met him – the distinguished Archbishop of the Russian Orthodox Church in Britain. Whilst still a student in Paris, Faith slipped from him. But one day, under pressure, he was persuaded to go to a lecture on "Christ and Christianity". The outcome can never be better told than in his own words: "I hurried home", said he, "in order to check the truth of what the lecturer had been saying. I asked my mother whether she had a book of the gospels. I expected nothing good of the reading, so I counted the chapters of the four gospels, to be sure that I read the *shortest*, not to waste time unnecessarily. And thus it was the Gospel according to St Mark which I read.

"I do not know how to tell what happened . . . Before I reached the third chapter, I was aware of a Presence. I saw nothing. It was no hallucination. It was simple certainty, that the Lord was standing there, and that I was in the presence of Him."

What other small book, I want to ask, could do that for such a reader in such a short time – and so lastingly? Unhappily, many of us who do Scripture reading are addicted to a few verses at a time; so that even a short gospel like Mark's never gets a proper chance with us!

* * *

Nor is this, even in our modern day, a solitary experience shared. The lasting power of the Living Lord can reach out in so many ways. Sir John Lawrence bears his own witness, brought up, as he was, in a liberal Christian family; reading Greats at Oxford, and as a student sharing a typical life of privilege, with its uncomfortable measure of questioning. Said he: "When the last glow of Faith had faded from the horizon for me, the world seemed by contrast inexpressibly cold and dreary . . . Then," he went on, "I considered the fact that if nothing was proved, equally, nothing was disproved: Ought I not to look again at Christian belief?

"So I got out my Greek Testament, and began St Mark's Gospel . . . When I was about halfway through, I began to ask myself, '*Who then was Jesus? Was He more than man?*'

"After that, I was over the top of the hill."

* * *

And I wonder did the widely-acclaimed British actor, Alec McCowen, have all this – or any of it – in mind, when he set himself to memorizing Mark's Gospel?

In the British newspaper in which he revealed how his famous programme came into being, he did not speak of it. He told only how he, a successful actor, had reached a place where he felt trapped in his profession. He needed a new challenge. He was used to learning lines – and as he looked into the future, he saw no problem as he set about learning and presenting the whole of this little gospel. It took him months to learn it, but at last he got it word-perfect.

And his presentation was an immediate success, where he appeared in auditoriums far and wide, on both sides of the Atlantic. Those of my own friends able to be present have never ceased talking of it. He appeared naturally enough, in slacks and sports-coat, as one with a Message very close to life! Nor was it, by any reckoning, just the novelty of it, as Stuart Blanch, Archbishop of York, was pleased to report, after Alec McCowen had appeared before the bishops assembled in Canterbury in 1978, for the Lambeth Conference. And there could hardly have been anywhere a more knowledgeable, more exacting audience, involving values far and away above a mere stage performance.

Writing of the overall effects of such an experience on himself, Alec McCowen was ready to say: "Whether or not you are 'a believer', it is impossible to study St Mark carefully, and not know – without any shadow of a doubt – that something amazing happened in Galilee two thousand years ago!"

*　　*　　*

"If" – as Dr William Barclay accepted, "Mark's Gospel was written shortly after Peter's death – the first gospel's date would be about A.D. 65. We could, at any rate, claim that *Mark's little gospel is the nearest approach we will ever possess to an eye-witness account of the life of Jesus*."

*　　*　　*

But, I have discovered, it is not for distinguished actors, bishops in conference, or learned scholars alone – diverse as their setting and daily needs may be. Mark's little book still holds something unique for ordinary readers, even young readers starting out.

I once had to cope with a youthful week-night club in the country. It was a church club, with an eager bunch of boys. It was hopeless to expect them to sit still for long, so I arranged for plenty of action. When it came to special Bible teaching, we dramatized Bible stories. We did "The Good Samaritan" for a start – and it was an immediate success. It took two of us to make a decent donkey that anyone could ride; a third to be the Priest who "passed by on the other side", and another the Levite, who did likewise. And all the rest of us were robbers – so we all had acting parts. We made a lot of noise, I must confess, but the story came alive! Another club night we did Joseph and his brothers, from the Old Testament, the young dreamer. Another time we did Paul, the missionary, in prison chains but keeping his courage up.

Then one of our lively youngsters turned eleven, and from somebody in his family got a Bible. Of course, I heard about it; with lightened eyes, my young friend reported it at the earliest opportunity: "I've got a Bible – got it for my birthday. And I've found Joseph; and in another place, David running for his life – but I can't get going with the New Part."

"What?", I questioned him, "The New Testament? Why, the best stories of all are there – 'The Good Samaritan' that we've done; and 'The Prodigal Son', and 'The Shepherd and his Sheep'." "Maybe," he had to answer, his face clouding, "but I can't get going with it – *too many begats!*"

Then it dawned upon me – he'd started into the New Testament, as was natural enough, with Matthew – where somebody begat this one, and somebody else begat somebody else – and he'd got all muddled up with "the begats". I wasn't really surprised, at his age!

But ever since, when I've had to deal with the owner of a new Bible – of whatever age – I've always said: "Don't start with Matthew – that's a Jewish book linking the Old Testament and the New – start with Mark. It's next in our Bible, but really first in point of time! And it's a young man's story! Start there – it's so full of lively words of lively doings: 'Straightway we went there', and 'Forthwith this occurred', 'and a young man came running'. Altogether, there are not so many 'sayings', as 'doings'. You'll enjoy it."

*   *   *

I don't lead a youth club these days, for as an author of many books I am drawn into other activities – letter-writing, research, typing, overseas travel, widespread public speaking, and, of course, reading. I welcome others' books as they come from their publishers, and in some rare instances am asked to write a Foreword to them, as lately, when a Scottish publisher found himself busy on a collection of meditations and prayers of my late, longtime friend, Dr William Barclay. How could I not take pleasure in doing anything I could for the work of one who had done so much for me and whom, in a book of my own dedicated to him, I had described as "One of the blessed who give without remembering, and receive without forgetting."

I now miss him greatly – not least, as when I recently found myself again in Scotland, where it had been our delight to meet over pots of tea, for talk of reading and writing. This time – when he was not there – I remembered how much he loved Mark's little book, as I rediscovered on reading through his S.C.M. paperback, *The First Three Gospels*.

He was not by any means the first to show such a love – students, preachers, writers, and ordinary folk – as some of us like to count ourselves, have done that. My good friend declared it "Christianity's contribution to literary types. It is without doubt the most effective literary form of religious expression that has ever been devised." And then he went on to say: "The gospels are not biographies." And this, of course, we discover for ourselves in time. "The gospels tell us nothing of the physical appearance of Jesus, nothing of His education, nothing except a few detached stories of the first thirty years of His life. Anyone who has ever tried to construct 'a life of Jesus' out of the gospel material will know just how far from being biographies the gospels are.

"The gospels are not memoirs, for in memoirs the story and the events and the characters all centre round the author, while in the gospels the authors might well be anonymous for all that they tell us about themselves. And yet the fact remains that in the gospels there is a vivid and unforgettable picture of Jesus as He was. It is interesting to note that in Mark we have the earliest surviving example of a type of literature which was the invention of Christianity."

If you ask me: "How is the Gospel of Mark to be most helpfully read?" the answer is: "*At least once – if not, again and again – at a single sitting* – as a clearly-packed, swiftly-moving story should be read. It can easily be done in an hour and a half, and reading silently, to oneself, in about half that time."

The little book consists, in the main, of a number of apparently detached incidents, in each of which Jesus does, or says, something significant. It would be a pity to think that having read or heard some of them from time to time, one knew it all. To read it as a whole, brings out its strangely cumulative power!

What's in a Name?

It strikes me strangely that I can say, "There was, of course, a time when there were no Christians in the whole world." And that was after Jesus had served a few years in the carpenter's workshop, and gone out to His public ministry. He had actually called young men to follow Him, but they had no name as a group – they were just followers, Peter, James, John, Andrew and the rest.

It would be a long time before they – along with the many others who joined them – would be known as "Christians". That would be a name, at first anyway, carrying a measure of derision. "But there never has been a better name", says Professor G.H.C. Macgregor, "by which to describe the followers of Christ. We are not Catholic or Protestant, liberal or orthodox. We are Christians. And in that descriptive name, we find the common basis of our unity." Dr Luke, in the New Testament Book of Acts, the first record of the Church, could write: "And the disciples were called Christians first in Antioch" (Acts 11:26).

But Mark was able to tell all of us who came later, about that first little company called to follow beside the Lake of Galilee (Mark 1:16-18). It was there, I remembered with great joy when I walked there myself, that "He saw Simon and Andrew his brother casting a net into the sea; for they were fishers. And Jesus said unto them, 'Come ye after me . . .' And straightway they forsook their nets, and followed Him."

They were soon joined by others, but were still nameless. Mark was only able to say, by the time he reached what is now the eighth chapter of his book: "He had called the people unto Him with His disciples" (Mark 8:34-39). "He

33

said unto them, 'Whosoever will come after Me, let him deny himself, and take up his cross, and follow Me'."

So it all began!

I was surprised when Dr Leonard Griffith, a distinguished modern preacher, who succeeded Dr Leslie Weatherhead at the famous City Temple in London, where I have worshipped often, chose as the title of his book *What is a Christian?* Was it possible that anybody had any doubt about that, all this long time after that name was first given? Would anybody buy such a book? (Later, when it reached my own country and was in my favourite bookshop, where I could leaf through it, I bought one. It was a book of sermons, the first giving the title to the whole book.) For a time, I found myself thinking that the preacher-author, like many of his fellows, was not "good at titles" – for surely, I felt, no one would find the one he had chosen very striking.

But a little while later, I was led to change my mind.

I went down from my hill-top home, "West Hills", to a hall in New Lynn, a suburb nearby, to hear a lecture by a young overseas author whose book we were all being encouraged to read *To Sir, With Love!*, by a young black teacher at a school in the East End of London, E. R. Braithwaite.

As he rose to address the crowded hall, his face shone with such cordiality that soon he commanded our whole interest. Late-comers continued to push in until seating being completely taxed, men gave up seats and some stood against the walls. Soon, we were all too warm, though our speaker seemed not to notice, having been brought up in crowded, warm, sunny Georgetown.

After he had told us of his loved cockney school, he made an opportunity for questions, if any cared to ask. Immediately, one here and another one there rose in friendly response. Then, a matron near the centre of the company made reference to something he had modestly reported as having done for his children in their needy lives, as "your

Christian deed". Very naturally, he replied: "But I'm not a Christian."

"But you are", she persisted, "if you do those kind of things to help – you're a Christian without knowing it!"

At once something within me said: "*But there's no such person*. And not all good deeds in this world, as a plain matter of fact, are done by Christians. *But nobody is a Christian without knowing it. Always a lively choice is involved!*"

(And I've not come upon a plainer, closer-to-life way of saying this – either to thoughtful young people or to thoughtless old ones.)

So Dr Griffith, I had to admit to myself, had indeed chosen a fitting title, and was set on essential truth! "We have our answer", said he crisply. "A Christian is someone who responds to the call of Christ. First and always," he then went on, "Christianity is a relationship to a person. In that sense it differs from great world religions like Judaism and Hinduism, and it differs from Communism and the other rival secular faiths that compete for men's allegiance today. All these direct our loyalty to a theological system, a code of ethics, a philosophy or an ideology, but Christianity alone directs our loyalty to a Person. Where Christ is, there is Christianity, and the Christian is a person who tries to be a follower of Jesus.

"We say 'tries' ", he adds, "because no one succeeds perfectly . . . It is by virtue of our relationship to Christ that we can call ourselves Christians." For He alone gives us Life!

*   *   *

Beyond that we Christians, of course, are as dissimilar as we can be – there is no one pattern. This is at once plain as we turn to the first chapter of Mark's gospel – and my comment on it, in this book that I have chosen to call *People and Places*.

Peter and Andrew were very different in temperament –
one of them early on full of "rush", the other as full of
"restraint", for all that they were brothers, and followers of
the one Master! (Mark seems, from his first chapter, set on
drawing attention to *supplementary service* – what my
dictionary defines as "a contribution designed to
complete".) And our Lord and Master, it is plain, works
that way still. In every team of workers for His Kingdom,
He seeks men and women of varied gifts and graces.

On that early occasion (Mark 1:29-35) the two brothers
were present when their Master was required to offer a very
intimate service. "When they were come out of the
synagogue," we read, "they entered into the house of
Simon and Andrew, with James and John. But Simon's
wife's mother lay sick of a fever, and anon they tell Him of
her. And He came and took her by the hand and lifted her
up, and immediately the fever left her, and she ministered
unto them."

Before long, service of another kind, present in a very
different situation, was required of them. No names are
mentioned this time – perhaps they all had a share in this
work. We read: "At even, when the sun did set, they
brought unto Him, all that were diseased, and them that
were possessed with devils. And all the city was gathered at
the door. And He healed many that were sick of divers
diseases, and cast out many devils; and suffered not the
devils to speak, because they knew Him."

Such service was exacting – and needed diverse gifts.
Little wonder that, Mark goes on to tell us: "And in the
morning, rising a great while before day, He went out, and
departed into a solitary place, and there prayed."

This was to prove, to the end of time, an essential secret
of His on-going service – and we have yet to grasp it, if we
are to prove useful servants of His everlasting Kingdom!

So we start off with a strong word from Mark – an
emphasis *very close to life!*

What's in a Name?

Not long ago I was struck by this glorious diversity symbolized for me in the Methodist place of worship and service in Whitechurch, Buckinghamshire. All too few of us, I fear, find our way there – and to its on-going message. For there, we are shown not only Mary the Virgin-mother, and the so dissimilar company of our Lord's first "followers", kneeling and bowing in the rapture of worship, but the first rugged missionaries of the Church – many of them to become martyrs, men and women both! But there, also, the likeness of Saint Athanasius, Saint Jerome, Saint Augustine, Saint Boniface, Saint Columba and Saint Patrick – all "followers" of the Living Christ whom we serve. And the great reformers there are of their company – and the preachers and great teachers. John Wesley is as fittingly remembered, if a little surprisingly standing by Cardinal Newman; and Dr Martineau; and the greatly-honoured missionary doctor, David Livingstone, is there; and Henry Martyn; and William Carey. Even so, one mustn't for a moment let oneself think that this covers all the diverse gifts and service offerings within Christianity. But here they witness together, in loving service of the Eternal Kingdom of our Master and Lord. Truth goes on growing, as Love goes on finding today new and relevant expressions.

To be a Christian becomes at heart, ever and ever, a more diverse *but personal and particular challenge!*

Family Affairs

I find myself wishing that we'd been told more about Mark's home and family life. We know very little really – only that he was the son of one Mary, a leading Christian in Jerusalem. And we are not told even that much about his father. It seems likely that by the time Mark came to be noticed, his father had been dead some time.

One thing is certain, that young Mark was in close friendship with Peter. Years on, in fact, the older man was very happy to call him "Mark, my son!" (Peter 5:13).

Dr Hastings, a noted scholar, lays considerable emphasis on the possibility that Mary was a widow and the head of her house. This is perhaps another reason why Mark didn't like being away from home too long, when, on that first missionary journey, at Perga he decided to go no further. When the extension of this hazardous undertaking was suggested, his mind was already made up, and back to Jerusalem he went. (Instead of charging young Mark with cowardice, as some have too easily done, we ought perhaps to be crediting him with a fine sense of family responsibility.)

We have no hint of any others growing up beside him in the family, though families in those days were seldom confined to just parents and one son. It seems unlikely that Mark's family was an exception; but Mark never speaks of brothers or sisters. Someone has suggested that he could have been a little shy about mentioning such family matters in a book that would go out beyond the home. But I hardly think this likely – certainly he was not shy of mentioning by name, in that same book, the brothers and sisters in Jesus' family (Mark 6:1-6). So I think it better to say that we just don't know about his family.

If it comes to the point, Mark doesn't mention the name of Joseph, Jesus' "earth father", and the general assumption is that he had died by this time. Can we reckon this to be the main factor in this young "carpenter apprentice" taking over the family business? We know that there were at one time in the family, young ones growing up, who needed providing for. The family wasn't by any stretch of the imagination affluent, as Mark's mother, Mary, appears to have been – they were just a small town carpenter's family.

But everything we are allowed to know about Joseph reads greatly to his credit and we are left with no question about his being a fine character. He could call himself "a son of David" – he was a man of religious values. "When Mary", we read, "was espoused to Joseph, before they came together, she was found with child of the Holy Ghost. Then Joseph . . . being a just man, and not willing to make her a public example, was minded to put her away privily. But while he thought on these things, behold, the angel of the Lord appeared unto him in a dream, saying, Joseph, thou son of David, fear not to take unto thee Mary thy wife; for that which is conceived in her is of the Holy Ghost. And she shall bring forth a son, and thou shalt call his name JESUS: for he shall save his people from their sins.

"Now all this was done, that it might be fulfilled which was spoken of the Lord by the prophet, saying, Behold, a virgin shall be with child, and shall bring forth a son, and they shall call his name Emmanuel, which being interpreted is, God with us.

"Then Joseph being raised from sleep did as the angel of the Lord had bidden him, and took unto him his wife: and knew her not till she had brought forth her firstborn son: and he called his name JESUS" (Matthew 1:18-25).

And there were other events – as when Joseph and Mary had to set off along the hot dusty road, with a crowd of others, to the census-taking in Bethlehem, only to find no accommodation worthy of the occasion. It was in its own way, another "awkward situation", for Joseph, but he carried his burden of anxiety as a good father. And that was not all. In all too short a time Joseph's sleep was again disturbed, to hear from an angel, "Arise and take the young child and his mother, and flee into Egypt, and be thou there until I send thee word: for Herod will seek the young child to destroy him" (Matthew 2:13). (Did anybody hear him say under his breath: "What next?" Here, alas, was the accommodation problem again! And what about the route? They can't, either of them, have been that way before.) But we read: "When he arose, he took the young child and his mother by night, and departed into Egypt." Let's hope it was a calm, kind, starry night. The little family is always shown travelling with a humble donkey, and Mary sitting on it hour after hour, holding the Babe entrusted to them – inexperienced parents.

But somehow they managed, together meeting the hazards of the road, and finding an answer to their needs when they got there. And they were there, the record says, "until the death of Herod: that it might be fulfilled which was spoken of the Lord by the prophet, saying, Out of Egypt have I called my son" (Matthew 2:15).

Eventually – and I've no idea how long that was – they got back home. And how thankful they must have been! One of our modern poets, Gilbert Thomas, has written a sensitive poem summing up his own reading between the lines:

> Who has not carolled Mary,
> And who her praise would dim?
> But what of humble Joseph?
> Is there no song for him?
>
> If Joseph had not driven
> Straight nails through honest wood,

40

Family Affairs

If Joseph had not cherished
His Mary as he should,

If Joseph had not proved him
A sire both kind and wise,
Would he have drawn with favour
The Child's all-probing eyes?

Would Christ have prayed "Our Father",
Or cried that name in death,
Unless He first had honoured
Joseph of Nazareth?

To the end of His days Jesus held in His heart many a thing that in the family He had learnt from Mary, during His boyhood in Nazareth. He watched her closely, as there she kneaded and baked the bread – never forgetting to put in the proper amount of yeast; and He watched her thread her needle, and sew on a patch, seated within sight of the whole family, long before He saw a tailor do as much for some one who perhaps did not have such a mother as theirs. And He told of these family things in His teaching-preaching moments. "The Kingdom of Heaven is like unto leaven, which a woman took, and hid in three measures of meal" – He even remembered the exact amount, which means that the Lad had watched intently. And as later the crowds hung on His words, it was plain to every woman present that He had a mother with an eye for a good patch. Mark too was struck by this, as Peter told it to him, and wrote it into his little book (Mark 2:21). "No man seweth a piece of new cloth on an old garment; else the new piece that fills it up taketh away from the old, and the rent is made worse."

And out of another family experience, Jesus added: "And no man putteth new wine into old bottles" – skins in those days – "else the new wine doth burst the bottles, and

41

the wine is spilled, and the bottles will be marred . . . , new wine must be put into new bottles" (2:22). Whether it had happened in His home in Nazareth, or in one of the neighbours', it would never be forgotten.

It is a grievous fact that there came a time when Jesus had to know Himself homeless, having to say: "The foxes have holes and the birds of the air have nests, but the Son of Man hath not where to lay His head."

*   *   *

Lately, travelling alone on a journey to Britain, I stopped-down en route at a foreign airport. I proffered my passport to a courteous, but soon confused, official at a proper desk at the proper time. (My passport, I should perhaps admit, answers the query "Place of Birth?" with but two names, without a comma: "Hope New Zealand.")

Running his finger along the line, the official then asked me: "What does this mean? 'Hope New Zealand' Does it mean that you hope you were born in New Zealand?" "Oh, no," I had to reply, "Hope is a place – a green, sunny, pastoral place in New Zealand; and I was born there!"

It was there that, early on, in the Summer grasses a group of us used often to play a game I liked. It was in turn telling one's "favourite word" for the day. There were plenty from which to choose – so that it might be "daisies", "rainbow", or "skipping". For me, it was more often than not one particular word: "belonging". That might now seem strange for a little girl, but it harked back to *my home and family*; to my tiny school, under the great trees at Hope; and then to my still tinier Sunday School, at the chapel at the cross-roads.

And in time it applied to worship, and to service in the worldwide Church, up through the years – till now it has more meaning than ever. And it is shared by some of the dearest, finest people I know. *It still holds – just "Belonging"*!

Whilst I was in Britain on that same journey, I happened upon a quaint old family-toast which took my fancy, so I dotted it down: " 'Ere's from we an' our'n, to you an' your'n; for sure there never was folk, since folk was folk, ever loved folk 'arf as well as we an' our'n love you an' your'n." Maybe!

Certainly family life is God-given. But also full of challenge!

Little Town of Memories

Like all writers, when Mark started his book, he had first to make up his mind at what point he would break into the vital story he had to tell. What kind of book was it to be?

Since it was not to be a biography, there was no reason why he should begin at Bethlehem, with the birth of the Child over whom the angels sang. He began his story with Jesus' young manhood, at the point where He went to the river for His baptism. Nazareth was the place that Jesus knew best – for years His home had been there, He had learnt His trade there, and by the time He left the carpenter's shop, He knew many of its people, if only as customers. And, of course, He knew those with whom He went to worship on the Sabbath. (Earlier, as a child He had run on the hills with His friends, the wind blowing in their hair, but those days had slipped behind by now.) But He bore the name of the little town long after He had left it and gone out into the wide world – "Jesus of Nazareth" folk called Him.

> "I think at Golgotha", wrote Edward Hilton Young,
> "as Jesu's eyes were closed in death,
> they saw with love most passionate
> the village street of Nazareth."

I have often stepped up into a bus and put my coins down for a ticket – but never was there a bus-ride in my life like the one I'm thinking of now. For my request was: "Two singles to Nazareth, please!"

Fortunately that morning, my home-friend, Rene, stood with me on the roadside, our backs to the Sea of Galilee,

when the bus pulled up. As we started off, I found myself
wondering whether the countryside had changed much
since the Lad Jesus and His family came that way. Of
course, the road surface nowadays would be kinder to
travellers; they never travelled by bus; and everything
then was much slower. But the undulating way with its
hills, and the sky overhead; must have been much the
same – with the same sun that we saw rising from the same
quarter.

Long before a visitor today gets to the little town, his or
her secret thoughts are bound to be of the Lad who, long
ago, grew up there. As a town, in itself it's not very
striking, and probably never was. Though beautifully set –
some sixteen hundred feet above sea level, it was not
historic enough even to be mentioned in the Old
Testament, or by Josephus the famous historian, or in the
Talmud. Some, even in Jesus' day, went so far as to count
it a little place of no reputation. (We get a hint of that in
the scornful retort of Nathaniel, when Philip sought him
out to say: "We have found Him of whom Moses in the
Law, and the Prophets, did write, Jesus of Nazareth."
And Nathaniel's query was, "Can any good thing come
out of Nazareth?"

Philip's wise response was: "Come and see!"

But the very nature of that dialogue dates it – nobody,
for a long, long time now, has spoken of that little town in
those derisory tones.

It was to this small town, home of Joseph and Mary –
nobody noticing – that a Divine message once came. And
with the years that passed, here, as in any craftsman's
place of work, father and son stood together beside a
carpenter's bench. At first, it must have been just play –
but He learnt, Phyllis Hartnell now reminds us, as,

> Silent at Joseph's side He stood,
> And smoothed and trimmed the shapeless wood,

And with firm hand, assured and slow,
Drove in each nail with measured blow . . .
Content to make with humble tools,
Tables and little children's stools.

But His days were not all work, as my Scottish friend, Dr
J.S. Stewart, with whom I shared a few hours lately,
delighted to remind me: "On almost every page of the
gospels there is something reminiscent of the youthful
Nazareth years when the sights and sounds of Nature
'haunted Him like a passion'."

And Mark does not forget to remind us of an opportunity
that came to Him, in later years, to pay a return visit (see
Mark 6:1). "He came into His own country; and His
disciples followed Him. And when the Sabbath day was
come, He began to teach in the synagogue: and many
hearing Him were astonished, saying, From whence hath
this man these things? and what wisdom is this which is
given unto Him, that even such mighty works are wrought
by His hands? Is not this the carpenter, the son of Mary, the
brother of James, and Joses, and of Juda, and Simon? and
are not His sisters here with us? . . . But Jesus said unto
them, A prophet is not without honour, but in his own
country, and among his own kin, and in his own house. And
He could there do no mighty work, save that He laid His
hands upon a few sick folk, and healed them. And He
marvelled because of their unbelief. And He went round
about the villages, teaching."

Dr Hugh Anderson is at pains to draw our attention to
the Greek words used. But he tries to add a note of hope –
that this story, which certainly did not conceal the harsh-
ness of Jesus' people's refusal to accept Him, might well
have brought consolation to early Christian missionaries in
days when *their message* was spurned.

I wonder, did Mark have a secondary reason like that,
for inserting this in his little book? We can't know. But we

do know that many still have a like experience. There is a
saying that "a doctor-son, in an emergency within the
family, can't even give a couple of aspirins to his mother."
"Sometimes", adds Dr William Barclay, in one of his
commentaries, "when familiarity should breed a growing
respect, it breeds an increasing distrust. Sometimes, we are
too near people to see their greatness."

*   *   *

I counted it a great privilege to go to little Nazareth; to visit
the Christian hospital there, pleasantly, airily situated on
the hill. On the way there – still on the level – I spied a local
mother, about the age Mary would have been when her
Jesus accompanied her to the same well, with a calabash, to
bring home water for the family. This lad looked about
twelve – the age when He went up to Jerusalem for the first
time. (When, having passed us by, these two were intent on
what they had come to do, I deftly snicked out my colour
camera. With garments like those worn centuries ago, my
resultant photo would fit into a Bible storybook without the
least alteration. So simple it was, so natural!)

I did not have a chance to go to the synagogue. But by
invitation I went to the home of the lady doctor, Dr Wilson,
across from the hospital. And a very cordial welcome that
was! Whilst she was a few minutes out of the room
preparing tea, my eyes fell upon her bookshelf where,
among others that interested me, I chanced to see several
of my own. (This moved me, instantly, to think that I had
something to bring to Nazareth!) Over our tea, we talked of
our travelling, and of our Faith. The Doctor had just
returned from leave, in her own country of Scotland.

And then she invited Rene and me to accompany her
down a little ankle-turning path, to where she and her
assistants would hold a clinic at midday. As we went down,
we gathered around us a handful of needy folk – an old

lady, partly blind, an old man with a stick, a young mother with a fractious baby, and a number of others.

Once over the doorstep, Dr Wilson introduced her two assistants: a young nurse, trained at the hospital on the hill, and a male dresser, also trained there. She briefly explained how they always paused for a few verses of Scripture, and to offer a brief prayer by way of dedicating "their skills and hands", in that place of healing.

Then, in the same gentle voice, she turned to me, to say: "Perhaps, today, you would lead us in our prayer?" And I did – counting it a very real part of the privilege of being in Nazareth, where Christ's ministry for wholeness of body, mind and spirit began.

*   *   *

Jesus, to the end of His "earth-days", held in His heart and mind what He learnt from Mary and Joseph, in that little Nazareth home. He held clearly what so unconsciously His mother taught Him about kneading and baking the bread for the family – never forgetting how much yeast she put in. And He watched her just as intently preparing to sew on a patch. In such a house there was no hiding good family undertakings, and He early learnt how fortunate they all were under that roof. And later, when He set off on His teaching, preaching and undertakings, His listeners benefited from all He had learnt at home, as He spoke to them in parables.

Lessons for life, learnt that way, would not be lost on home-keeping people.

*   *   *

But we must not think of Nazareth as "a little, slow, sluggish place" – not at all. It had its life. For, as my friend Dr J.S. Stewart reminded me as we sat in Edinburgh,

"High up above little Nazareth, one of the world's great roads went by." "From end to end of the Empire", he had written in one of his books on my shelves, *The Life and Teaching of Jesus Christ*, "the great highways ran, triumphs of Roman engineering . . . built to carry Caesar's legions to every corner of his dominions, and in time, the missionaries of the Gospel came marching; and everywhere their message spread like wildfire. Christ's men could never have evangelized the world as they did, if it had not been for the Roman Roads."

And rich, exciting caravans passed occasionally, almost at Nazareth's door. As the saying came to be accepted: "Judaea was on the way to nowhere, and Galilee was on the way to everywhere."

Seeing Eyes

Long ago, when first I left my home-land on world travel, I carried a new passport which said that my eyes were "hazel". It surprised me then, and it surprises me still. After many more journeys the newest passport in my care still says the same about my eyes. I would have thought it more important for that official document to be able to claim that I had "seeing eyes".

I can't think of any possession more important for a traveller. And Mark, the writer of the earliest gospel, would, I think, agree. He wrote into its proper place there a penetrating question that Jesus, the Master, put to His early disciples: "*Having eyes, see Ye not?*" (Mark 8:18). They were travellers, too, of course, even if only on foot, and over a much more limited area.

Of their Master – and ours – Gilbert Thomas says today:

> He spoke two thousand years ago –
>   The Word was flesh to His own age.
> But later generations know
>   Only the printed page.
> His message? Dons have disagreed,
>   And blood has flowed because divines
> have lacked the homely wit to read
>   His smile between the lines.

Yes. And let us add, "His glorious awareness between the lines"! Mark was happy to tell that "As Jesus passed by, He saw . . . " (Mark 2:14). And what did He see? The immediate answer for us is, "He saw Levi, the son of Alphaeus sitting at the receipt of custom." And more – He saw that he hated his job, and all its unhappy implications.

But Mark was happy to add that this led, that very day, to a telling divergence in Levi's life. For in answer to Jesus' call "Follow Me!" . . . Levi did arise and follow Him!

And as He went on His way, Jesus saw many another, with a problem all his own. For instance, there was one fellow, "sick of the palsy" (Mark 2:1-12). That was in Capernaum, but he was fortunate to have in that place where he suffered, four good friends. And they got their heads and hearts together in a plan to help him. They would set him on his mattress, where in any case he spent most of his time, and, one at each corner holding tight, they would take him to Jesus. And to all looking on, it turned out to be an exciting event, *for those four friends had to take the roof off, to get him there*. There was such a crowd, and there seemed no other way they could manage, although the friends had not, until they were faced with the situation, even thought of such a thing.

But it worked! "And immediately" – and this was a great "moment" for the use of that favourite word – "he arose, took up the bed, and went forth before them all insomuch that they were all amazed, and glorified God, saying: 'We never saw it on this fashion.' " I should think not! But then, Love – especially shared by four good friends – is very inventive, isn't it!

*   *   *

Jesus saw also the natural beauty of the commonplace wild flowers, and the birds above the fields. He saw the signs of the threatening storm, so disturbing to the mother-hen and her little brood. Even closer to His own heart, He saw the children at their games – weddings and funerals – in the market-place. And it didn't stop there – on another occasion He saw Mary Magdalene, a woman whom many others would be glad not to see, darting from the shade of one sleazy street to another, seeking something special in her life.

Nothing escaped Him, particularly anyone with a need! In our day, when few of us are as observant, an unknown writer says:

> The simplest sights He met,
> The sower flinging seed on loam and rock;
> The darnel in the wheat; the mustard tree
> That hath its seed so little, and its boughs
> Wide-spreading; and the wandering sheep; the nets
> Shot in the wimpled waters – drawing forth
> Great fish and small – these, and a hundred such
> Seen by us daily, yet never seen aright,
> Were pictures for Him from the book of Life,
> Teaching by parable.

But a young poet of our beautiful country, New Zealand, felt he had to say this:

> I knew a man
> Who – raving on "the view",
> Broke with his clumsy feet
> A spider-web
> Starry with dew.
> > Donald McDonald

We don't know the colour of Jesus' eyes. Nobody – not even Mark, with his love of detail – thought to tell us that. But I could well be right – the colour of eyes has always mattered less than their power "to see"!

Courage to confess shortcomings is not always as common as could be wished for. I can only think of one person, of my day, ready to admit as much, and in unforgettable lines:

Seeing Eyes

Life blew trumpets of colour,
    Her green sang in my brain –
I heard a blind man groping
    "Tap-tap" with his cane;
I pitied him in his blindness,
    But can I say, "I see"?
Perhaps there walks a spirit
    Close by, who pities me,
A spirit, who hears me tapping
    The five-sensed cane of mind
Amid such unguessed glories
    That I am more than blind.

Anon

Good Soil and a Handful of Seed

When I was last over for the English spring – with keen hopes of spending time out of doors – the weather was not kind, and there were few sunny days.

But I did manage to make my way, as I always do when in London, out to Kew Gardens, although only on the very last day before I was due to leave for home. With a lifelong fascination for seeds, as the result of my country upbringing, I don't like to be denied that London pleasure. Since Kew Gardens first were Kew Gardens, I am told, seeds from all over the world have been brought there by travellers from obscure places, as well as by known naturalists, and by garden-lovers. These seeds have been identified and planted in what is now its glorious near-three-hundred acres, with every species of flower, shrub, and tree plainly marked for identification. And now, however modest one's seed knowledge, one may wander at will, by "stately avenues, and sequestered walks, and lakes, ponds and palm-houses, conservatories, glorious flower-beds, rockeries, museums, classic temples, and lawns, and herbaceous areas", as my knowledgeable, ageing notebook goes on, adding them up.

Because there are some parts that, even on my six or seven visits, I've not had time to walk in, I entered this time by a different gate, reaching immediately an unknown area. But in doing this, I missed the familiar lithe figure of the Sower standing, as I love him, with his seed-bag slung over his shoulder, representing one of the most exciting and hopeful undertakings in our whole world: *sowing seed!*

Jesus has a lasting story about that, which Mark passes on in chapter 4:1-20. When Dean Stanley was travelling in the Holy Land, he came upon a part near the Sea of Galilee which was an almost perfect picture of this loved parable of our Lord's. "There", said he, recounting that moment, "was the undulating corn-field, descending to the water's edge. There was the trodden pathway running through the midst of it . . . hard with constant tramp of horse and mule and human feet. There was the rocky soil which distinguished the whole of that plain . . . There was the rocky ground of the hillside protruding here and there through the corn-field, as elewhere throughout the grassy slopes. And there were large bushes of thorn, springing up . . . in the very midst of the waving wheat" (Stanley, *Sinai and Palestine*, p. 425).

"The central idea of the story", he adds, "is that, the seed being of one quality, the crop depends upon the character of the soil."

It is a favourite story still, and any one of us happily studying the Parables of our Lord finds himself or herself spending some time on it. It seems, at first, a simple story – though with the experience of years, the more we bring to it, the more there seems to be in it.

"The sower sows the word", as one distinguished scholar, Dr C.H. Dodd, says. "It is not suggested that Christ Himself is the Sower. Any faithful preacher is the Sower." I would add, "Any faithful Christian – layman, or laywoman, teacher of a class of children, leader of youth and – to include myself, as I think one must always try to do in interpreting the Parables helpfully – any Christian writer, and public speaker wherever folk are gathered to listen, turning their faces hopefully towards one."

Dr Dodd goes on realistically: "He will find much of his work wasted. Some hearers" – and I add, "some readers" – "will never grasp the truth effectively. Others will be discouraged by difficulties, beguiled by prosperity." But still the Doctor is able to add – as you and I, nearing its end, may quote, from v.13: "Know ye not this parable? . . . The sower soweth the word. And these are they by the wayside, where the word is sown; and when they have heard, Satan cometh immediately" (there's that word again, but here it carries a sorrowful content) "and taketh away the word that was sown in their hearts. And these are they likewise which are sown on stony ground; who, when they have heard the word, immediately receive it with gladness; and have no root in themselves, and so endure but for a time: afterward, when affliction or persecution ariseth for the word's sake, immediately they are offended.

"And these are they which are sown among the thorns; such as hear the word. And the cares of this world, and the deceitfulness of riches, and the lusts of other things entering in, choke the word, and it becometh unfruitful."

But let us take courage – and keep on. It doesn't end there. Says the parable: "And these are they which are sown on good ground: such as hear the word, and receive it, and bring forth fruit, some thirtyfold, some sixty, and some an hundred!"

And with wonder, let us not fail to rejoice in that!

"This business of broadcasting the truth has its wasteful, unproductive side", another modern commentator, Dr Robert E. Roberts says in his book *The Present Message of the Parables* (Epworth Press). "You waste a lot of energy and a lot of seed. 'The seed' is good. Nothing wrong there. But the soil – that is what tries the sower's temper. Shallow, stony, thorny – and the result will be nil except in the patches of rich deep soil. It is well the disciples should know this.

"Jesus knows it", he adds, "and keeps at it." His motto is, as ours must be:

> Sow in the morn thy seed,
> At eve hold not thine hand;
> To doubt and fear give thou no heed,
> Broadcast it o'er the land.

(Hymn)

And if for any reason this should not be clear enough, Dr Roberts finishes: "What are we to do?" And he brings forth his own answer: "*Do as Jesus did. Broadcast it. Keep on keeping on*. It is no use thinking of Jesus as a popular idol leading a waiting people into the joy of the Kingdom. However attractive that idea, it is simply not true. All that we are up against in human nature, He was up against. He looked facts in the face, and kept on! He sifted the crowd with His swift mind, and He knew that He was sowing seed – precious seed – on paved streets, in weed-choked gardens, in all sorts of impossible places – lavishly throwing away that which, if the ground were good, would multiply a hundredfold!"

Many of the pharisees were plainly "wayside hearers", with minds so hardened that the truth could not enter. And it is tempting to say, at times, the same of some whom we know – but we do get some surprises! This, through the years, is my experience! Sowing is glad service, after all. With a hasty glance, we can't always judge the soil aright.

And every time I read Mark's little gospel, or go to Kew – and see that fine, lithe figure with his sack of seed, his arm outstretched in the act of sowing – *I am challenged afresh!*

Dual Blessings

Only Mark, it seems, spared space to tell of the blind man healed quite differently from others. Most were healed instantly and completely – but this man *progressively*, and I am glad to know his story.

I find myself wondering why the other recorders making up "The Synoptic Gospels", Matthew and Luke, missed him out. Was it, perhaps, that they felt that his story reflected poorly on the healing powers of Jesus? Or could it be that with blind men and women all about them, they felt there was little newsworthy in his story? Certainly blindness – even to this day common in Palestine – was part of the daily scene.

When visiting Palestine myself, I have spent a lot of time in the company of blind people. One Sunday in Jerusalem, at worship in the cathedral, I was struck to see the choir composed entirely of tall blind girls, so when the service was at an end, I sought out an English woman from the congregation to ask about them. We had all been invited to make our way to the cloisters at the close of the service, for cool drinks.

I was fortunate in my choice, as she was none other than the wife of an English Methodist minister, the Rev. Leslie Farmer, who had served in the country as a chaplain during the war days, and was at that moment leading a London church party through the Holy Land. When we were introduced, I greeted him: "Are you Leslie Farmer of the two books on my shelves? I'm Rita F. Snowden, of the books from the same publisher, likely on your shelves". And we shook hands with an instant sense of "belonging".

"What are you two girls doing this afternoon?" was his

first question, when I brought my friend forward and introduced her. "We're going out to Bethlehem, on a visit to a Home for little blind children. I had something to do with it, when I was here, as a chaplain. After we've spent time with them," added our new-found friend, "telling them stories, and sharing cold drinks, listening to their singing, we'll go on for the evening meal, to another home, where we are to be guests of a company of delightful blind girls.

"Will you come?"

It was a Sunday never to be forgotten!

As we drew near, the little blind ones spilled out along the path to greet us, especially our leader, whom they called "Uncle Leslie!" And Rene and I were introduced as having come to visit them, from a little country away on the other side of the world. Since we were English-speaking, the little ones sang a hymn for us in English, offering the only one they knew by heart, one that our children at home sing year by year at Christmas: *O little Town of Bethlehem!* And there we were, in its midst – in its spirit of Christlike love and compassion.

And that afternoon of joyous Christian sharing blessed us! After tea and more chat and singing, a kindly woman with a car drove us back to our Cathedral lodgings.

"Blindness", James Hastings had already assured us, "is all too common in this land of our Lord. Apparently," he added, "only two forms of blindness were recognized in Bible days – that which arose from the ophthalmia so prevalent, a highly infectious disease, aggravated by sand, sun-glare and dirt . . . together with that due to old age." Interestingly, in his *Dictionary of the Bible*, the Doctor had gone on to draw attention to this blind man mentioned by Mark (Mark 8:22), *the man whose recovery was gradual*. Mark's words about Jesus, on that occasion, were: "He cometh to Bethsaida; and they bring a blind man unto Him . . . and He took the blind man by the hand, and led him

out of the town." (Resorting then to an accepted treatment, He asked him presently if he saw ought? And he
looked up and said: "I see men as trees, walking.")

That can only mean that he wasn't yet fully healed –
things were still out of focus, out of perspective!

"After that", Mark goes on, "He put His hands upon his
eyes, and made him look up: and *he was restored, and saw
every man clearly*." Wonderful!

Altogether, this complete healing had taken some time.
(We note the consideration of Jesus – He had no concern
for His own public credit as a healer. He might, surely,
have healed the unfortunate fellow there and then, in full
gaze of the crowd – and have reaped a reward of gasping
amazement. But it is likely that the man before him had
already suffered enough at the hands of the crowd – most
did, having no choice but to sit in their darkness, and beg by
the wayside. Jesus, wherever possible, showed a loving
respect for a sufferer's right to privacy, as He did here;
when the man was completely healed He sent him home –
"not into the town" (v.26). The curious, the quizzing crowd
was no place for him. Jesus wanted to spare one who had
suffered much, from suffering more – he was not to be a
side-show for anyone's interest, or noisy news-gathering.

It was a healing which must have required some *patience*
because it was gradual; but for all that, when he was healed,
he was *fully* healed! He no longer saw "men as trees,
walking". Things were, once again, properly in perspective!

And still – as we who have suffered lengthy illness, and in
time, renewal, well know – healing can be granted either
progressively or instantaneously. That, like many an
experience in our life here, is in the hands of God.

I wonder why Mark felt he wanted to tell this healing
story in his book? Yet our sense of perspective must be in
things spiritual, as well as in physical wholeness (Mark
10:47-52). Jesus asked: "What wilt thou that I should do

unto thee?" The blind man said unto Him, "Lord, that I might receive my sight." And Jesus said unto him, "Go thy way: thy faith hath made thee whole." And immediately he received his sight, and followed Jesus in the way.

* * *

Illustrative of wholeness, progressively or instantaneously experienced, not in bodily joy, but in the realm of the spirit, are the complementary stories of young Timothy and St Paul. Timothy grew up simply, naturally, thanks to the loving, fostering care of his grandmother, Lois, and his mother, Eunice. These were both of them fine women of real religious spirit (2 Timothy 1:5).

Saul, in contrast, came all of a sudden into a shattering conversion experience on the Damascus Road! (But they never argued, as far as we know, which was to be lastingly counted the "better way".)

There are still two ways of wakening – with the gentle light of the sun finding its way into one's room at an early hour, or later, even much later, being loudly roused by a knock on the door.

The first way was Timothy's coming to wholeness, the second, Saul's. A modern writer has put this second way very plainly:

> A desert way,
> A burning sun,
>   And – Saul,
> A heavenly voice,
>   And – Paul!

So Small, but Important!

Mark seemed happy in his human values, and made room for a gentle story of little ones being brought to Jesus (Mark 10:13-16). He wrote: "They brought young children to Him, that He should touch them" – though surprisingly, he doesn't actually say that it was the mothers who brought them. Until this moment, I've never paused to question this point, but there is nothing more natural than that, if anyone should count the little ones important enough to break in on Jesus' time and consideration, it would be the mothers.

To support that actuality, most of us have from our early years been brought up to sing the little hymn, which says assuredly:

> When mothers of Salem,
> Their children brought to Jesus,
> The stern disciples drove them back
> And bade them depart;
> But Jesus saw them as they fled,
> And sweetly smiled, and kindly said:
> "Suffer little children to come unto Me."

I can believe that Jesus and the mothers were one in this – and probably alone too, as certainly few others did then show concern for children. Indeed, in ancient Greece and in Rome, Aristotle showed a situation which unbelievably caused him no embarrassment as he reported it. "Master and slave", said he, "have nothing in common – a slave is a living tool, just as a tool is an inanimate slave." And Varo, as damningly, when summing up human values among the Romans, stated in his treatise: "there are the *articulate*,

comprising the slaves indoors and out, and the *inarticulate* –
comprising the cattle, and the mute, comprising the
vehicles."

The lot of the child, small and defenceless, was for
centuries grievously overlooked. In Greece, where small
families were favoured, children were an inconvenience,
and when the family had reached an acceptable size they
were left to die of exposure. It was a hard world for young
and tender things.

A Roman father held the right to destroy a babe at birth.
After the first girl was born into a family, Imperial Rome –
always anxious about its army – required fathers to bring up
only healthy males.

But we needn't go back as far as Greece and Rome; in
life the greatest service was done to little children by the
coming of the Christ Child to Bethlehem. It was a new
revelation of human values! So small He was, that His
mother wrapped Him in swaddling clothes, so human and
defenceless, that she laid Him in a manger bed; so Divine,
that over Him at birth the angels sang. Later, in His
ministry, Jesus "set a child in the midst", and in that, did
one of the most far-reaching things in all history!

Mark, of course, was aware of all this, and when he came
to write his gospel, he set down the charming story of the
mothers and their children seeking out Jesus (Mark
10:13-16). "They brought young children to Him, that He
should touch them; and His disciples rebuked them that
brought them. But when Jesus saw it, He was much
displeased, and said unto them, Suffer the little children to
come unto Me, and forbid them not: for of such is the
Kingdom of God. Verily, I say unto you, Whosoever shall
not receive the Kingdom of God as a little child, he shall not
enter therein.

"*And he took them up in His arms, put His hands upon
them, and blessed them.*"

Such values, alas, have not been all at once, easily, or universally accepted. You and I are embarrassed to have to remember the Penal Law of England at the time of Wesley. There were no less than a hundred and sixty crimes for which men, women *and children* could be hanged. And that's not so long ago – Wesley lived between 1703 and 1791. In those days, in England, you could be hanged if you picked a pocket for more than a shilling; if you grabbed goods from someone's hands and ran away with them; if you took from a store wares valued at more than five shillings; if you stole a horse or a sheep, or even ensnared a rabbit in a gentleman's estate. Charles Wesley, brother of John, actually wrote in his "Journal" that he had been in a prison preaching to fifty-one felons waiting to be hanged – and one of them was a little boy of ten!

Travelling in the North of England, I learnt that there still exists in one place a plaque commemorating a mining disaster, which reads: "In the year 1832 the Lord terribly visited the colliery of Robert Clark, and the above-named were called to meet their Maker." Appended is a list of twenty-three names. The shattering significance of that plaque is that all who lost their lives on that grim occasion were under the age of nine years!

Above ground, conditions were often lamentable – children of six or seven were assembled at the beginning of a work day, and marched off to the fields, to pull roots, pick up stones, or spread manure till dark released them from their miserable exhaustion.

Did no one in authority read Mark's little story of the children, in his chapter ten? Even in our world today, there are still "brutes" who do not recognize that Jesus values little children. They certainly have not read that chapter we have been focusing on, in Mark's ageless gospel.

* * *

So Small, but Important!

"Our century", says the great present-day leader, Cardinal Suenens, in the spirit of the New Testament, "has discovered interplanetary space, but it has scarcely begun to explore the space which separates us from one another. It has built gigantic bridges across rivers, but it has not yet learnt to bridge the gap that separates people from people. Our century has discovered nuclear energy, but it has not yet discovered the creative energy of peace and concord."

Astonished and Amazed

I can't, of course, share here everything for which I owe a debt to Mark. My indebtedness is too great – and it keeps growing. At best, I can but hint at the rich life he felt led to write about, revealed in the living Lord of Life whom he served. Each reader of Mark's gospel, I feel, finds herself or himself won over again and again to some new reality.

Dr A.B. Bruce liked to say of that little book that "It was written from the viewpoint of loving, vivid recollection" – and that "its purpose, from the beginning, was to support a glad, on-going Christian life."

It is good to remember the impact that Mark's Master made upon the mind and heart of those who heard Him. He was not just "a good man" – He had powers never before, or since, placed by God in one living on this earth. As He moved amongst people, the awe He evoked was remarkable, and later it was always in Mark's mind.

In one place Mark wrote: "They were astonished at His doctrine" (1:22). And almost immediately, in 1:27, he added: "They were amazed." (And such phrases are sprinkled throughout his record, as you will discover.) Nor was this only the reaction of men and women who heard Him as they gathered for worship in the synagogue; but it happened outside too, as they saw Him heal, and deal with milling crowds, some of whom assembled out of curiosity.

And it was true also of His own disciples, sharing with Him countless hazards as they journeyed. In Mark 4:37 ff you will be asked to appreciate their human alarm, as "there arose a great storm of wind, and the waves beat into the ship, so that it was now full . . . and He arose and rebuked the wind, and said unto them, 'Why are ye so fearful? How is it that ye have not faith?' . . . And they said one to another, '*What manner of man is this, that even the wind and the sea obey Him?*' "

Hardy fisherman that many of them were, they never came to accept Him casually (Mark 6:51). Later, Mark shows us this in another experience at sea, when He joined them unexpectedly, "and the wind ceased; and they were sore amazed in themselves beyond measure, and wondered."

Dr William Barclay was moved to say, "*No one tells us so much about the emotions of Jesus, as Mark does*. He was – in my words – to those who met Him, by no means 'A wooden character in life' – for all that He was 'a good one'." As early as chapter 1 (v.41) Mark tells us: "Jesus moved with compassion, put forth His hand." The needy one, in this experience, was, we are told, *a leper*. That was remarkable in itself, that a religious leader should show a readiness to draw near to such a person.

"Compassion" is not a word much used in our general conversation today; but in New Testament times it was common, and meant much. Indeed, our scholars rejoice to tell us, it was one of the most wonderful words in its original Greek language, in which our New Testament came into the world. It means, in the kindest, most tender sense, "heart-sorry". And this was the word used again and again to describe the reaction of Jesus. One commentator tellingly claimed that when Jesus was moved by compassion, He always did something to help. At times, it was to help many! Mark says of one early occasion: "Jesus withdrew Himself with His disciples to the sea; and a great multitude, when they heard what things He did, came unto Him.

"For He spake to His disciples, that a small ship should wait on Him because of the multitude, lest they should throng Him.

"For He had healed many; insomuch that they pressed

upon Him for to touch Him, as many as had plagues. And unclean spirits, when they saw Him, fell down before Him, and cried, saying, 'Thou art the Son of God' " (Mark 3:7-11).

*   *   *

Drawing attention to other expressions of His relationship, Dr Barclay liked to remind us how, on one occasion (Mark 6:34): "*He was moved with compassion* because they were as sheep not having a shepherd [the crowd] and He began to teach them many things. And when the day was now far spent, His disciples came unto Him, and said, This is a desert place, and now the time is far passed; send them away, that they may go to the country round about, and into the villages, and buy themselves bread: for they have nothing to eat. He answered" – in the true spirit of compassion, typical of Him – "Give ye them to eat. And they say unto Him, Shall we go and buy two hundred pennyworth of bread, and give them to eat? He saith unto them, How many loaves have ye? Go and see. And when they knew, they say, Five, and two fishes." And so we have Him taking charge of the situation – "making them all sit down by companies upon the green grass", as Mark likes to tell us; and he is the only one of the gospel scribes who adds that delightful natural touch. It helps us to see them, in all their varied colourful garments, in companies like flower-patches spread out – "in ranks by hundreds, and by fifties" (Mark 6:39-40). Five thousand of them, benefiting from His compassion!

Again, Mark gives us a word picture of the Master's inmost spirit, in relation to the very young and innocent (Mark 9:36). "And He took a child and set him in the midst of them: and when He had taken him in His arms, He said unto them, Whosoever shall receive one of such children in My name, receiveth Me: and whosoever shall receive Me, receiveth not Me, but Him that sent Me." There was something so special – so compassionate and tender – about a man who could immediately instil confidence in such little ones.

Then in the next chapter, as it now appears in Mark's book, is the further account of His handling of children which we mentioned a few pages back (Mark 10:13-16). And reading what Mark must have taken pleasure in reporting, we feel that Jesus must have been to the children an attractive, trustful, joyous person – or such fearless relationships would never have developed. He could never have been to them, as so many pictures by mediaeval artists made Him out to be – a placid, sad-looking man, sitting very still with a little group of angelic looking children around Him, behaving in a way that real children never do. The suggestion that He stroked their heads – a thing most children dislike – and talked some sort of improving talk to them, is only one degree worse.

It must be right to think that His interest in children was natural since there is a New Testament record of Him watching them playing funerals and weddings in the market-place. I believe that Mark is meaning to say, when he writes, "when He took them up in His arms", that they were quite at ease with Him, perhaps even pouring out their little string of questions, chatting away freely. A child soon knows what kind of person he is talking to. Any kind of talk that causes the smile to die on his lips, not to say frightens him when he finds himself so close, may well be some kind of religion let loose in the world, but it cannot be called Christianity – it lacks the natural strength and winsomeness of Jesus Christ. Any stiff, critical, or gloomy attitude that makes no place for youthful playfulness, and is afraid to draw a deep breath of fun, has nothing that will win a friendly following. And children are quick to know it.

When Mark, with a light in his eye, set down these and other word-pictures of Jesus, he knew he had got his record straight and honest. These lovely gifts came from God, the Creator of trees and flowers and ponds, of music and funny things like little ducks and puppies, that added up to a sense of liveliness, needed on some rough parts of our journey on earth!

Clearly, we see now that the Master's joy, and its naturalness – as Mark liked to hear of it among the common people – was something vastly more than mere good nature. No man could possess His sustaining spirit – unless He was sure both of God and of Himself!

And it is likely that Mark has no greater secret to share. How else can we live in this kind of world?

Blessed Barnabas

Most of us find a fascination in names. Do you? For me it started away back in my first little school, under the great trees, at Hope. One morning, a little "new" girl came, who told our teacher, when she brought out the register, that her name was "Birdie". But Teacher couldn't believe it – nor could we children already seated at our desks, in readiness for our day's learning.

"Is it a nick-name?" Teacher asked. "No, it's my name", the little girl answered, "and I've always had it." "Have you no other?" pressed Teacher. "I must get you to take a note home to Mother – and please bring me an answer in the morning." And it was so. Thereafter, we soon settled to an acceptance of it. And "Birdie Tasker" remained to play and work with us for years.

* * *

Young Mark had two names, as Dr William Barclay liked to remind us. In Acts 12:12 there is a reference to "the house of Mary, the mother of John, whose surname was Mark", and it is repeated before the chapter is out (v.25). "And Barnabas and Saul returned from Jerusalem . . . and took with them John, whose surname was Mark." And two chapters on, in Acts 15:37, we hear it as plainly again! "And Barnabas determined to take with them John whose surname was Mark." "In Palestine", writes Dr Barclay, "it was regular practice for a man to have two names, one a Hebrew name, by which he was known to his friends and family circle, the other a Greek name, by which he was known to the wider world of business and of public life. (So we have Simon who was called Peter, and Thomas also called Didymus.) In this case, John is the Hebrew, Markos the Greek – with Marcus in Latin – the public name."

Mark's cousin Barnabas, mentioned here, was one even more favoured: his name was blessed with the meaning "*Son of Encouragement*" (Acts 4:36; Revised Standard Version). Who amongst us would not be happy to bear a name whose acknowledged meaning was "Son of Encouragement" – or, if its equivalent could be, "*Daughter of Encouragement*"? In this world in which we live, encouragement is often hard to come by. Mark plainly knew himself blessed to have such a cousin; without him, the Church in the world today might never have had his little book in view of Mark's "upset" on his first missionary journey when he went home – save that on another occasion, "Barnabas and Saul returned from Jerusalem . . . and took with them John, whose surname was Mark" (Acts 12:25).

Whatever his good cousin, Barnabas, felt about the situation, here he was in his famous role as "encourager". Without him, who knows whether Mark would have risen to be the man he became – not only a fellow servant of the Church, but the writer who gave us this gospel! Blessings on Barnabas!

* * *

The church where I regularly worship celebrated its hundredth birthday some time ago, and I was privileged to take an active part in a first celebratory service, "The Sacrament of Holy Communion", and in its very last, "A Festival of Talents and Tongues". That evening, we had a display of paintings, pottery, flowers and music that we had offered to God. And I was asked to speak briefly as well, on a theme selected for me by the committee – that of "Encouragement".

Positioned near the lectern where I stood to speak, was a local, and very valued, young family orchestra. Their presence led me to think of music, in relation to regular worship in the congregation, and the chosen theme.

Since I was their age, I had entered into many rich experiences of "encouragement" – but musically, my lack was such as to spread a note of warning to others, young parents and members of families present.

About the time when my little twin sister and I were nine, we had no piano in our farmhouse, no musical instrument save a "fiddle" and an accordion our father had acquired before he married. Years after that, came an early Edison phonograph, with a very impressive tin horn like a fluted convolvulus, which occupied a little table in a corner of the "best front room". But still, there was no piano – our good parents always meant to get one, when we came of an age to learn. (And at that point, I was very close to my theme!)

We lived in the green countryside, a mile or two from the nearest shopping village where a teacher might be found, and where we could "start to learn". Money wasn't very lavish on a "husband-and-wife farm". But as the days passed, we were blessed with birds, fields, and four-legged creatures!

Then came a day when our parents drove off to the nearest town (Nelson, thirteen miles away) but night brought them back with nothing to show for their effort, music-wise.

Still the passing of the season meant that another opportunity did come – and returning from school one day, we were to find that our father and mother had brought home a piano in the back of the farm-wagon. By the time we arrived, our father and a good-hearted neighbour had pulled down the side fence near the house, to get it in.

Well, it was a great moment – we all looked at it admiringly. Our father said, "It's plain, but good!" And we always believed everything our father said. It had no brass candlesticks, as Miss Palmer's piano had – we children supposed that was what he meant. We were allowed to invite our teacher to tea, to try it. A great moment that!

But so much hung on whether a music teacher could be found!

After a week or two, our father came home from the village, where he'd gone to get the mail, to say that he'd heard of a piano teacher, and had knocked on her door. She turned out to be somebody he'd known in his early growing-up years, but with whom he'd lost touch. She was a widow now, with two boisterous boys to support, and an aged mother.

"Yes", said she at last, she could "take" us – and, being two of us, *at a reduced rate!* She would bike across to our farmhome, on an agreed early evening, once a week!

Alas, we soon found that our teacher didn't always come "early". Again and again we'd have to get up, put coats on over our nighties, and one by one each have a music-lesson. More than that, there were times when she might be even later, coming straight from milking the house-cow – and I could tell, sitting beside her on the piano stool. More than that, she always came to our house on an outrageously squeaky bicycle, that hadn't, we could tell, met with a can of oil in months!

I was a somewhat logical little girl, I suppose, and I argued it out with father and mother at tea-time: "Any lady music teacher who can bear to ride such a terrible loud bicycle", I claimed, "can't show me how to make the beautiful music sounds I want to make!" (And I'm afraid a little doubt was sown in the minds of my parents – though they didn't say anything. But soon it must have dawned on all concerned that there was no future for me in scales, by heart, and a little "Book of Pieces", and "Czerney's Exercises". Week by week, as she came later and later, the heart dropped out of things! I didn't really, at any time, want to learn the piano. I loved my father very much, and he played the "fiddle" – and I wanted to play the "fiddle". I liked doing the things he did!)

"But no," my parents both answered me patiently, sensibly – "learn the piano first – and how to read music, and count time – it will help, if ever you come to the 'fiddle'. We can see about that later." Just then, as I knew, there was no teacher for the fiddle anywhere – and we did have a piano teacher! But there was no encouragement in that for me, though my little sister was getting on with her effort.

And I gave up practising eagerly. At last, as the third term came to its weary end, I was allowed to give up.

Years later, when I was finished with primary school, and ready to go on to college, my proficiency certificate secured, a phenomenal storm, with flooding, suddenly washed away all the cultivated topsoil of our farm; and many of our animals and chickens, not to mention our wheelbarrow full of kindling wood I'd brought to the back-door. Our railway line too was soon gone – and much else! We had to come off the farm, as did others, so we moved to the village – and I went to business. Instead of going to college, I started a correspondence course, alone at night. My father was a very quiet man those days. He got himself a job – and never had a farm of his own again.

At the end of six years at business, I studied to sit exams, and was received as a candidate for Deaconess Training, in the southern city of Christchurch. During my last year at business, I had hunted out for myself a violin teacher a little more than six miles away, who from now on, once a week, would come to the village by train. She could "take me" – but I would have to wait for a vacancy. It was a long, dispiriting wait, but I did, at last, make my way to a little room by the library, at lunchtime, once a week. However, when I was still little further on than the "squeaky stage" that budding violinists seem destined to pass through, the time came for me to travel south, for my first term of Deaconess Training.

When, in answer to an eager letter, I learnt that there was no music room where I was going to live and study, I knew to my loss that I must leave my "fiddle" at home. Had I attempted to practise in my room upstairs, my fellow students might well have thrown me out into Latimer Square, across from our front gate – or in greater desperation, into the city's shallow River Avon, a little further off!

So, to this moment, I have music in my heart – but none in my hands. And it's a sad admission!

* * *

But I never now fail in my thanks for a rich life experience of reading and writing, and all the encouragement that has reached me there! And never now do I forget the day when I came upon a fellow reader and writer, an eager Nature lover and fine Christian, Grey of Fallodon. In one of his unforgettable moments he wrote: "I wanted to be made to feel two inches taller. And I found this that I needed, through the visit of a friend!"

"That's it!" "*We each need a Barnabas!*" I am continually saying under my breath!

Joined Closely

Although the two kindly ladies who for years ran "The Corner House" in the Cotswolds have gone, I have been back to Burford – it's a wonderful part of England to visit in the Spring. Again and again, when work for my publishers was at a close, I made my way there, and I shall always be grateful to those two ladies. They directed me hither and thither, and I made some "rich finds". Usually a supporting lunch-packet saw me setting off, and my little car served me well in covering many miles. Parking occasionally, I walked on with my haversack.

One "find" was tiny Widford Church. As I made my way to it on foot across wide, green country spaces, lazy cows lay half in the sun, half in the gentle shadow of the great trees. Once at the church I walked into history, and, the door being unlocked, I entered. I hadn't seen a person to speak with all morning, which was quite an experience in itself, after many weeks of addressing crowded meetings, travelling, and sleeping in a fresh bed every night – though I enjoyed it all while I was doing it. Now, I needed refreshment of mind and spirit, and I found it that morning. Inside I came upon an ancient piece of tiled floor, which at one time had belonged to a Roman house. Its pattern fascinated me; and it somehow seemed so right that it should be there.

In his gospel (in what is now chapter 1 verse 29) Mark presents the rightness of a lasting link between Church and Home. Mark's words belong to the ministry of Jesus, as He moved around. He had been having a "very busy time". But now He was with friends, and Mark started his report, as he delighted to do, with one of his favourite words:

"Immediately, His fame spread abroad throughout all the region about Galilee" (verse 28). And then came what I recalled especially, as I stood hushed, in tiny Widford Church: "Forthwith, when they came out of the synagogue ["they" being Jesus and His disciple friends] they entered into the house."

Strictly speaking, it was friend Peter's house, as Mark must have remembered, and his mother-in-law was sick. (But there was the Church and the Home, tied very closely!) And I said to myself, alone in all that holy quietness, it should always be that way – not only when sickness is present, but all the time!

By the time that our Lord's crucifixion, resurrection and ascension had become part of human history, Paul found himself writing letters to support fellow Christians. A typical one began: "Greet Priscilla and Aquila, my helpers in Christ Jesus . . . Likewise *the church which is in their house*" (Romans 16:3 and 5). Again, on another occasion Paul sent an encouraging letter out to other Christian friends (Colossians 4:15): "Salute the brethren which are in Laodicea, and Nymphas, and *the church which is in his house*". Just as natural as that – joined closely!

And again, in what in our Authorized Version is "The Epistle of Paul to Philemon" (verses 1 and 2) comes another such greeting: "Paul, a prisoner of Jesus Christ, and Timothy our brother, unto Philemon our dearly beloved and fellow-labourer, and to our beloved Apphia, and Archippus our fellow-soldier, *and to the church in thy house*; grace to you, and peace, from God our Father and the Lord Jesus Christ."

Just as natural as that – joined closely!

* * *

With the passing of the years, when Christian buildings for worship were first raised under the wide sky some were very small, some large, some simple in architecture, some magnificent! And that is how it still is today, in churches where men and women assemble with their families, and later return to their homes. Countless numbers of us have been taught, strengthened, and supported in this wide-spread experience.

But we have to admit that there are also countless numbers – especially in the more favoured countries, in what is called "the West" – who have grown careless of this centuries old privilege, so that the churches that grace cities and countrysides are not now as full at the hour of worship as once they were.

As a regular reader of newspaper headlines, does it strike you that many of them are related to some depth of family and social laxity? I have spent some years of my life in social service among the lawless in our city and community, in prisons and places of detention. I do not claim to be able to put my finger on any one cause of loneliness or lostness, or, working backwards, on juvenile delinquency and lack of glad respect for persons young and old, their ideas, and their property. Where do young people earliest and most effectively learn human values? These days even sports clubs and schools don't seem to be enough. How often, indeed, do our daily newspapers carry pictures of "street-kids" and of gangs, of woefully damaged schools actually wrecked or burned by young people themselves, of assaults and burglaries, as well as of all kinds of vulgarities.

It's not very long ago that I grew up in a pleasant countryside, and a home where we never had a key to either front or back door – and I didn't know anybody who did.

It's not many years since I travelled our land from end to end, driving a special book-van and caravan – one woman alone. For almost six years, the seasons round, each night I returned to my caravan to sleep – parked in camping grounds, on roadsides, or on a sandy beach, sometimes in a farm paddock in the company of cows or sheep; in scenic reserves; between tall buildings doubly dark after business in our capital city and in other cities; and, at the other extreme, spending three nights in a country cemetery. That was in a country place in the north, blessed with a fine Maori name, Kaukapakapa. I had thought, as I drew near with my twenty-four-feet length of equipage, that I might park down by the trees and houses, but they'd had a week of rain, and when the church steward met me, he had to tell me that such was impossible. "The place is sodden", said he. "If you get away down there, with the weight of books you're carrying, you'll never get out. I've taken it upon myself to mow the grass up here, just off the road beside the church. You'll be speaking here!" Then he asked politely: "Would you mind sleeping three nights in the cemetery?"

"Not at all," I answered, and immediately moved my van and caravan in off the road without further questioning – only offering thanks for his attention to the grass!

*   *   *

But today no youngish woman alone would think of travelling through the land in that manner, and no Church bookstore would ask her to do it. Things have changed. A pity! Police reports, T.V. and radio reports remind us daily of the risks. All over the Western world, this seems to be so. A pity? No, a thousand pities! How has it come to be?

I can only think that if the Church and the Home, with all that they have to offer, all the time, for the needs of "body, mind, and spirit", *were closely tied together*, it would make a great difference in human values and behaviour!

In the Neck

I've long known that some words in the Authorized Version of the New Testament do not now carry the surface meaning they once did. Times change with the centuries, and words change too. This has arrested me, as I have reread some of the Master's words recorded by Mark 9:42; A.V. "Whosoever shall offend one of these little ones that believe in me, it is better for him that a millstone were hanged about his neck, and he were cast into the sea." Oddly enough, I was just confirming for this book the fact that "little ones" does not only mean "children", but can also apply to humble, little-regarded people in the community, and that the "millstone" here is not a small stone of a handmill (as in Matthew 24:41) but the huge grinding stone of an ass-driven mill. In this instance, "Death", declares *The Interpreter's Bible*, "would be inescapable."

But "a neck is a neck" still, and is unchanged – even "a pain in the neck". I learnt this and much else, when I recently ceased typing for a time, so that with a fresh cup of tea, I could listen to a radio service, "Faith for Today", by Bryan Paynter, who was talking, coincidentally, about various pains in the neck. He plainly had knowledge that I didn't possess – and I was fascinated. Later we talked of it over the 'phone, and he wrote me a letter, graciously allowing me to quote him.

"When people say that something's 'a pain in the neck'," were his first words that arrested me, "they usually mean something more than a minor irritation . . . After all, a neck is essentially something your head sits on. It lets you move your head around quite a wide range of at least half a circle, and by moving your eyes around as well, you can look about you a full circle.

"The muscles in your neck act as guy ropes to keep your head balanced; if they get sore and tighten up, you find it's hard to turn, or even to keep your head in a comfortable position. It's even worse if one of the nerves in your neck gets pinched or irritated – this is painful in itself. But then the muscles tighten up to protect you by stopping movement of your head, so you're working overtime, and their painful fatigue makes the nerve pain worse.

"It's a real 'pain in the neck', as anyone trying to back a car down the drive will know. But there are lots of causes of neck-pain," the speaker added. "A common one is a sort of locking of a small joint. It swells, and irritates the nerve next to it. I've also noticed that people who've lost all or most of their sight seem to be prone to neck-pain, because not having to look at things means the need to turn the head lessens.

"I note in the Bible", he went on, "that people from time to time have been called a 'stiff-necked generation', and I've wondered how that particular expression arose. The Greeks had a word for it, and it meant 'hard-necked'. Its meaning is usually given as stubborn or obstinate. I suppose it came about as an analogy because when another is trying to get you to change your mind about something, you set your neck hard and stare out across the horizon; the last thing you want to do is to turn your head, and look your persuader in the eye – you might give in!

"You can take this further", he added. "Perhaps, if you refuse to look about you, and have some narrow-straight-ahead point-of-view that never considers either the faith or the personality of others, you eventually find that your neck's got stiff, and you end up by not being able to look about you, even if you want to.

"You can also relate this to the way we tend to see in others the very failings we dislike in ourselves: the good old judgemental attitude that arises from what the psychologists call 'projection' – seeing your own traits in others – usually, the undesirable ones.

"Jesus was very well aware of this; and He knew how much more we can magnify these traits in others. From His workshop experience as a carpenter, He described it as 'seeing a speck of sawdust in someone's eye, without noticing the plank in your own' – the piece of 'four-by-two' we might say . . .

"On the other hand, we might sometimes find good reason not to condemn in others what we might be tempted to do in ourselves. This is the 'At least, I never do *that*' attitude. I might occasionally lose my temper, but at least I don't gamble or cheat. I might gamble, but at least I don't cheat. I might believe that 'business is business' but at least I don't steal.

"I think that whatever technique we use to justify ourselves to ourselves – whether the 'projection method', or the 'at least I never do that', it's because we're stiff-necked, and can't look around. Our eyes are locked on a far horizon where some mirage of our own personal standards deceives us into considering them valid for everyone else.

"There's a story that Aesop, the fable-teller, was walking from Athens to Argos, when he met a man going the other way. The man wanted to know what the Athenians were like. 'Tell me first', said Aesop, 'what the people of Argos are like.' The man said, 'They're disagreeable, mean and selfish.' Aesop said, 'Well, you'll find the people in Athens just the same.'

"Later, Aesop met another man going from Argos to Athens, and this man asked, 'What are the people in Athens like?' Once more Aesop said, 'You tell me first what the people of Argos are like.'

" 'Oh! They're very pleasant – kind, friendly and hospitable.' Aesop said, 'I'm happy to say you'll find the people of Athens just the same.' "

A nice ending to a radio-talk!

But you and I are left with the need to work out our Lord's grim warning about the millstone – and the terrible "pain in the neck" awaiting some evil-doers! But Mark felt he had to report it.

Early or Late

It was early. The darkness was yet velvety black, but I raised my arm, and switched on the light. It was a quarter to four – and very still. But it was yet too soon to rise.

At this, my other arm reached out and I took down *A Book of Hours*, a slender, beautifully produced gift from a minister friend in Canada. Representing "a serene and mature faith". When at home I keep it near on a well packed shelf. Its author is a Quaker woman. A "Note" on its opening page reminds me that "Books of Hours" first became popular during the late Middle Ages. Written and designed for private devotions, and illustrated by exquisitely detailed drawings, highly individual in character, no two books were exactly alike.

"This contemporary Book of Hours", said its author, Elizabeth Yates, with gratitude plain enough to her publishers, Vineyard Books, Inc, Noroton, Connecticut, "is patterned after one of its forebears although inspired by all of them. It is a book designed in and for our own time."

The Master, Jesus, used often to rise for prayer in the early hours. As Mark's gospel reminded me (Mark 6:46) he asked help with the dispersion of a crowd of five thousand that He had fed: "And straightway He constrained His disciples to get into the ship, and to go to the other side before unto Bethsaida, while He sent away the people. And when He had sent them away", we read, "*He departed into a mountain to pray*." (This was at the latter end of the day, though Jesus often made His way out early – I can't believe that even Peter knew of every occasion.)

And he never outgrew prayer, nor was it ever for Him an accepted obligation, but rather a privilege. It was not just that God would give Him things, or that in a crisis God would do things for Him – a view that all too many of us His disciples today are inclined to take. It was chiefly that for Him prayer was His way of communion with God, as essential as the air He breathed. One unknown scribe has set it down like this:

> My God, is any hour so sweet,
>   From blush of morn, to evening star,
> As that which calls me to Thy feet,
>   The hour of prayer?

> (Anon)

"At its best, when we pray", says Alexis Carrell, the scientist, sharing the life of our demanding world, "we link ourselves with the inexhaustible motive-power that spins the universe." And more – we link ourselves with the all-wise, all-loving Father of our Lord and Master Himself, who is unfailing in every situation, and to the very end. When cruel men had done their worst to Jesus, and hanged Him upon a Cross, even there that relationship of Love and Trust was unspoiled, and He could pray: "Father, into Thy hands I commend my Spirit."

And it was enough. In the fullness of time, He arose triumphant over Death itself!

It is the same all-loving, all-keeping, glorious God with Whom we have to do, early or late, in prayer. As Dr Harry Fosdick of our day so tellingly said: "Prayer is not crying to a mysterious individual off somewhere; prayer is not bouncing the ball of one's own aspiration against the wall of one's soul, and catching it again. True prayer is fulfilling one of the major laws of the spiritual world and getting appropriate consequences."

It is following in our own setting, the so-human, so-Divine Lord and Master Whom we choose to follow. At any time, and in any situation, it can be as real as He knew it to be. One does not need to wait for an appointed time, nor to possess a particular prayer book, or "Book of Hours", much less to be able to summon up from the depths of one's capacity, beautiful words. That we should be wrapped about with Love, Faith, and Reality in this world in which we are set to live, as He lives, is all that matters. To us will come, not one expected, or unexpected experience outside the glorious adequacy of Communion.

When the Master taught His first disciples to pray, He did not say: "If you pray . . . set about it like this"; He said "*When* you pray . . . " for living the kind of earth-life they were set to live, He knew that they would! The time might sometimes be that of an early morning, or even a crisis situation, when they knew not what else to do, as when Peter, of a sudden, found himself in danger in the sea.

The saintly George Herbert was heard to say: "He that will learn to pray, let him go to sea." The seas were as mighty then as now, all human undertakings fraught with hazard. This we know for ourselves when we reach out in prayer, as for some solid support when we feel ourselves falling, or failing. We cannot avoid these experiences. I once prayed in a howling gale in the Atlantic, when we had fourteen days and fourteen nights of buffeting, when nobody could get up for meals; and on the second Sunday we had two S.O.S. calls to ships in distress. And I can't think how often I've prayed when called to visit folk in prison, at the request of a family in despair or shame. Many a night through the years of social service in a great city, I've offered silent prayer beside the cot of a little one in hospital, when some modern last resort treatment has been put to the test. What we call "a crisis prayer" is very real then – for all that the answer of the All-loving, All-knowing, Ever-present may have to be "Yes", or "No", or "Wait!" And we have to summon our readiness to accept it as the very best.

We have also, of course, to realize that prayer as a whole experience is not just to bear us from crisis to crisis. It needs to be considered as essential as breath – and as constant. There is no true way in which we can live without communion with God. The words of the old saint can never be forgotten: "*Thou has made us for Thyself, O God, and our hearts are restless until we find our rest in Thee!*"

But for many of us prayer is often scamped. We go for days, and weeks, and more, and never pray. No wonder that we are sometimes obliged to face the fact that our religion is not very real. Some leave prayer to the fag-end of the day, and then occasionally find themselves falling asleep over it. Others don't even attempt that much, save when they want something for themselves. They do not realize that Communion with our Creator, Saviour and Sustainer, is at the very heart of prayer. Prayer is discovered to be so much more than "nudging the arm of the Almighty"; the proper spirit throughout is not "Do *for* me what I want", but rather "Do *with* me what You want!"

We do not know how often in His earth-life Jesus prayed, though there are many gospel references to His going away into some quiet place for that good, strengthening and refreshing purpose. And we mustn't think of His Communion with His Father as being always a solemn relationship – sometimes it must have been full of joy, full of thankfulness and praise! It's a pity that artists and illustrators who offer us books and cards for our religious life, seem always to show Him solemnly cast down, even seeming to be under strain. There must have been times when it was like that – but I am just as sure that there must have been other times when His heart was full to overflowing with holy gladness. I know how it is, even in my own faltering experience. Communion, like a warm, sweet, strong human friendship through the years, varies greatly. So does prayer, over-flowing most naturally in praise and thanksgiving! The mail comes, with an airletter or card, bringing heart-lifting news from a dear friend! Or near at hand, a flower bursts into colour and fragrance in one's garden, after much digging and desiring. And as the early sun of God's giving falls, one's praise rises to Him! Or a record one has sought for months is at last secured, and its beautiful liquid tones flow through one's lounge, and will do many a time again, when a music-loving friend calls. Or a book, on which one had spent hours of one's precious life, planning and writing, eventually comes through the post, well-packed, and bearing a word of sincere satisfaction from one best able to assess its worth! If this could be counted in any way a prideful moment, it must be admitted that for its author, it proves a very humbling experience, but one of joy and praise too – and prayer bearing these lovely qualities rises easily to God!

Our Master never wrote a book, or played a musical instrument, or dug in a garden, as far as we know – but there must have been times when, sick folk, crippled, or blind, were healed, or truth being at last grasped by some little group of listeners meant that His heart truly overflowed! And like the rest of us, one by one, He wanted to get away from the crowd, and in Communion with God express praise and thanksgiving.

Along with intercession for others, these are amongst the richest and most rewarding moments of Prayer!

> For the beauty of the earth,
>   For the beauty of the skies,
> For the love which from our birth
>   Over and around us lies . . .
>
> For the joy of ear and eye,
>   For the heart and mind's delight,
> For the mystic harmony
>   Linking sense to sound and sight . . .
>
> For each perfect gift of Thine
>   To our race so freely given,
> Graces human and divine,
>   Flowers of earth, and buds of heaven!

(Hymn)

He Could Not Be Hid

When I found I was to stop over for five days in Istanbul, I was excited, although I knew nobody there, nor, for that matter, anyone who had ever been there. I did know that it was an ancient city, for a long time carrying the name "Constantinople", the Christian city of Constantine, but that it was no longer the capital of Turkey. When I was still a student, away back in 1923, it had been required to give way to Ankara, and I ought to have heard a little more about it at the time – after so many centuries, that change must have been a great upheaval.

Now that I was to visit Istanbul in person, I lifted down my weighty *Encyclopaedia Britannica*; but it tipped into my lap so much history that I had no possibility of scribbling even a quarter of it into my modest travel notebook, much less of storing it in my mind.

On arrival, the very first of the ancient city's buildings I entered was the noble, sky-searching mosque, the one-time Church of St Sophia. Since it was no longer a Christian place of worship I was required to walk in silent and shoeless. An unmatched creation of Byzantine architecture, its oval-ended nave reached out two hundred and thirty-four feet in width. It seemed immense though figures in themselves are usually bothersome. This central spaciousness was served by four great piers, with arches supporting a mighty dome a hundred and ten feet in diameter, rising into the sky a hundred and eighty feet overhead! There is probably some impressive architectural term for all this, but I didn't discover it. What I write here is supported by remembered eye-knowledge, and the notes I hastily jotted down. In any case, it hardly seemed fitting that someone from the "ends of the earth" should, silent and shoeless, be juggling with pencil and paper in such a place.

Soon, having rescued my comfortable shoes and restored them to my feet – in itself, bringing back my traveller's confidence – I moved out, pondering what I'd experienced and written in my notebook.

Since the ancient building's immensity had been commanded to serve humanity's needs of a different and unexpected kind, most of its Christian symbols and inscriptions had become overlaid. A long time earlier a Christian traveller had encouraged me to look for a striking representation of the ascendent Saviour Christ, His arms out-reaching in blessing. That, I was told, was now showing through the one-time covering of wall paint. Humbly I sought it out, and as I stood before His gracious likeness, words from Mark's little gospel spoke to me: "*He could not be hid!*" (Mark 7:24)

And I turn now with great interest to my commentaries and travel books. One of the first with anything to say on the issue assured me that "thousands of sermons have been preached on these words of our title." Maybe! Though I must confess that I have never heard one. May I ask how many you have heard? And I have never written of the meaning I find in these beautifully simple words, in any one of my books.

Mark used these words that, in translation, come unforgettably, once we have given thought to them. They are part of a happening that took place in a very unusual setting. (Not in Istanbul, I need hardly underline, but in "the borders of Tyre and Sidon" . . . an area that may well have seemed as strange to our Master, as Instanbul did to me.) Thinking over it, my late friend Dr William Barclay wrote: "When this is seen against its background . . . it becomes one of the most moving and extraordinary incidents in the life of Jesus." Does that make you immediately curious to know more about that background?

As a start, let us look at its geography. "*He arose*", to use Mark's words, as they come to us, "*and went into the borders of Tyre and Sidon*." This was an area with a history reaching back a very long way. It was a rocky, somewhat inaccessible area. Tyre and Sidon were both centres of life in Phoenicia. Tyre not only boasted a famous harbour, but an equally famous fortress. It was claimed that the first sailors ever to steer their ships by the stars, came from Tyre and Sidon. Hitherto, those who set out to sea had, for safety's sake, to hug the coast, and to lay up when night fell. But in time, Phoenician sailors daringly found their way about the waterways of the Mediterranean, and through the Pillars of Hercules. Sidon lay a good distance from Tyre, and, like Tyre, had a natural breakwater.

Capernaum, Dr James Hastings reminds us, was regarded as "the headquarters of Christ in His Galilean ministry, after His rejection at Nazareth." Here, among many other recorded happenings, He taught in the synagogue on the Sabbath (Mark 1:21), He healed the man with the unclean spirit; and, among other miracles, the man sick of the palsy, who took up his bed and walked (Mark 2:2-12). Here later Jesus also taught humility to His disciples (Mark 9:33-35) which was, indeed, a miracle too, seen by one writer in our day as "the greatest miracle He ever performed – remaking the spirits of men in themselves so dissimilar, and getting them to work together."

Having made the journey from Capernaum to Tyre and Sidon, Jesus was in Gentile territory. For us, all this long time afterwards, it is difficult to grasp the difference that resulted in that chasm between Jews and Gentiles. Many scholars besides Dr William Barclay find themselves, in their own language, saying as much: "When this incident [of the Syrophenician mother and her earnest pleading for her sick daughter] is seen against this background . . . it becomes one of the most moving and extraordinary incidents in the life of Jesus" (Mark 7:24-30). But we have to be careful in thinking of the daughter as a small child – the diminutive in which the story reaches us, some scholars suggest, may only be a form of endearment – but I can't see that it greatly matters. The same tender term is sometimes used of a girl of marriageable age. More important here, I think, is the fact that the young person healed is the only one in his gospel whom he designated unmistakedly a Gentile. That is not to be passed over.

Distraught, the mother sought out Jesus – not only in that unlikely gentile setting but when He was seeking privacy. "He could not be hid." What surprises me most in Mark's account of the happening is Jesus' immediate answer – seeming at first to suggest that she has no claim on Him. His reference to certain persons as "dogs" shocks us – it seems so out of character. "But the story", as Dr Barclay adds, "must be read with insight . . . To the Greek the word 'dog' meant a shameless and audacious woman; it was used exactly with the connotation that we use the word 'bitch' today. To the Jew it was equally a term of contempt. ('Give not that which is holy unto the dogs') (Matthew 7:6). "The word 'dog' was, in fact, a Jewish term of contempt for the Gentiles."

But even in this seemingly shocking and unsympathetic answer, we see as the incident advances that He sends her home to find her daughter healed, and the truly loving spirit of Jesus "cannot be hid" (Mark 7:24-30).

Was then His "shocking" answer His way of testing her earnestness? Or was it, as another scholar suggested, that at that point Jesus was not yet fully persuaded of the nature of His own mission – was it only to His own people, or was it also to the Gentiles? Or was it that, in the end, He might show up the more His secret desire, indeed, His loving determination, to show that His Gospel was for all. Somebody else suggests that He was only jesting with the woman in His reference to "the dogs", or "the doggies", as yet another suggests in a desire to soften the impact of that difficult retort. But surely such an explanation is totally out of character with Jesus; we cannot be allowed to think of Him jesting with a poor mother in such distress. As "He could not be hid" in His physical, earthly sense, so we can confidently say, *He could not be hid in His glorious all-pervasive spiritual concern!*

Wherever we find ourselves in need of His help, in a familiar place or in the strangest of strange places, we may be sure of His living, loving presence!

Essential Solitude

One only has to leaf through Mark's little gospel to realize that the Master led one of the *busiest* lives ever. His total earth ministry was not long as these earth-years are counted, but Mark has no sooner set himself to tell of Jesus' Baptism at the hands of John, His fore-runner, than he has need of the liveliest words in his vocabulary. "And straightway", he records, "coming up out of the water, He saw the heavens opened, and the Spirit like a dove descending upon Him: and there came a voice from heaven saying, *Thou art My beloved Son, in whom I am well pleased*" (Mark 1:10-11).

"And immediately" – and he is using another favourite word, to introduce concisely the desperate forty days His Master spent in the Wilderness – then on, to use again the word translated for us as "straightway", in other event-packed verses (Mark 1:18-20 and 21).

He has called his first disciples, there beside the lake shore, and out of the midst of their net-mending, they have taken leave of their old father, Zebedee, and are ready to be off. Soon they are being led along the shore on the way to Capernaum. They may have been there many a time before – but this was different! Their young Master, Whom they hadn't yet had time to get to know as well as they needed to, was already engaged in a ministry of healing and speaking.

"And straightway on the sabbath day He entered into the synagogue, and taught. And they were astonished at His doctrine: for He taught them as one that had authority, and not as the scribes. And there was in their synagogue a man with an unclean spirit, and he cried out . . . And immediately His fame spread throughout all the region round about Galilee . . . " (Mark 1:21-23,28). That meant people, people, people – people to be healed, people to be taught, people by day and night, coming with questions they had hugged to themselves for a long time. And there were His disciples always about Him – strong young men, and very strong-minded some of them, who needed to get to know each other, and whose temperaments had to be matched up into a team. One here, and another there – as time proved – was over-ambitious. It must have pained Mark to have to record, of a later visit they made to Capernaum, a question their young Master had to put to them: "What was it that ye disputed among yourselves by the way? But they held their peace: for by the way they had disputed among themselves, who should be the greatest. And He sat down and called the twelve, and saith unto them, If any man desire to be first, the same shall be last of all, and servant of all" (Mark 9:33-35). They were slow to learn the principles and spirit of the Kingdom of God.

The very fact that Mark wrote such an account into his gospel at all stands proof of his honesty – it would have been much better to have been able to write that they were eventually "perfect men". They never were, and Jesus must have found them trying at times, along with the responsibility for doing the Father's Will in the world that rested on His shoulders. And there was all the stubbornness and evil of mankind; the blindness of many religious leaders; the poverty of many people; the spiritual, the bodily and the mental suffering of the crowds "like a sheep without a shepherd".

But He had a wonderful secret, as One living on this earth both human and Divine, and Mark breaks into that first chapter of his using the words "straightway" and "immediately". "And in the morning, rising up a great while before day, He went out, and departed into a solitary place, and there prayed" (Mark 1:35).

In London in 1937 it was my privilege to look upon the countenance of a somewhat frail man who did just that. Out of the unexpected massing of family and royal circumstances, a great burden came to be placed upon the shoulders of this man, already serving in many ways. But this was different. As it happened, He was blessed with faith and with the love of his family; but it had to be a move made within the full gaze of the world and affected by a great fog of gossip, infused into the life of common people by way of the media. (I left my home country not knowing of the public shifting of such a burden, but before reaching London I learnt through the ship's radio that there was to be a Coronation on a fast-approaching Spring Day. A longtime friend, who knew the date of my arrival, fixed accommodation for me covering the set date.

Like countless others who chanced to be in London at that hour, or, hearing the news, turned purse and personal plans upside-down to attend, I got to my seat near Buckingham Palace at a few minutes to four that morning. There was a long wait – but it didn't matter. Many had slept out overnight, in their slight sleeping-bags and water-proof coats. One couple near at hand, I saw, were just getting up, having spent the hours of darkness there, a Big Ben alarm tied on to a nearby plane tree.

It was altogether a wonderful day that for thousands of us stretched into singing and cheering when the royal personalities came out onto the palace balcony as the stars roofed the scene.

But it was something individual which our new King, George VI, chose for himself the night before, that has remained longest in my memory – for me the greatest event of that total Royal Event. When kingship was first thrust upon him there was no hiding the hope that he might avoid it, but as days went by, he knew it was not to be. Reading between the lines of history, we can see how his strong sense of duty was reinforced by a deep personal religion.

On the night before the Coronation, the Dean of Westminster received a telephone call from the future King. "I want to come to the Abbey tonight", he announced. "Certainly, Sir. I will be there to receive you."

"No, don't do that", he replied. "I want you to see that the postern door is left open. I wish to come into the Abbey, and *I wish to be alone*." So that night the King kept a vigil of prayer at the altar where on the morrow the pomp and circumstance of Coronation would take place. It was, of course, the best of all preparations for what awaited him. In the solitude there, he found what he always counted on: a stabilizing and courageous contact with God.

Dr Hugh Anderson's commentary on Mark's gospel holds striking words that are to the point here. We are given a little word picture of Jesus "in the morning, rising up a great while before day, and going out to a solitary place, to pray!" "Jesus' withdrawal to solitude and prayer", he says, "points up His dependence on God, the only source of His authority."

*   *   *

It may not be authority so much as guidance, and the strength to do His Holy Will joyfully and tellingly, that you and I seek. It does not make any real difference whether we seek out His presence within solitude, in the light of early morning, or in the soft velvety darkness of night. It's the solitude that proffers us the help we cannot get in a crowd or in a place of many demands. This can be your secret and mine – we don't have to be a king to find it.

I like to remember another hero of my days, Dr Edward Wilson, Christian doctor, painter far above the average, and friend, who went south to the great white frozen spaces with Captain Scott, and shared that little tent with him when Death laid hold of them.

In the days when they moved south by ship, Dr Wilson

was discovered to have climbed weekly up into the airy solitude of "the crow's nest", there, at an appointed time, to share his period of Bible reading and prayer with his wife at home, far off in England. Morning or night, it made no difference.

It's the solitude which counts – prayer together jointly points up dependence on God.

I once spent some hours with an old lady in her simple, beautiful little home, set in a garden in the south of New Zealand, as book-loving friends had asked me to call on her when I got to that part of the country. It was a lovely sunny afternoon, and she was out in her garden tending her roses. She snatched off her sketchy old hat, and said, "Come inside, and see my Polar pictures!" And there they were, on her wall – choice originals. When I exclaimed at sight of them she told me that Mrs Edward Wilson had given them to her, when she had lived with her whilst he was away in the Antarctic.

We took up his published books. I had identical copies at home, and knew them off by heart. Opening them now, one and another in turn, we read aloud our favourite passages. But always my kindly hostess came back to the one about prayers in the crow's nest – "That's my favourite!" she said, again and again.

And it's mine, too!

A Living Memorial

Mid-morning, however busy I am, I make a quick dash out to see what the post has brought me. This morning, my Spring overseas mail brought a letter from a dear English Quaker friend.

Away back in the 1930s, my friend Rene and I were asked by the British Y.W.C.A. to run an international camp for young women, since we had a goodly experience of camp-life. But before the time came, and we arrived at a well-known college in Sussex, lying between the sea and the Downs, we knew it was going to be fun. We had first to deal with language difficulties. At Grammar School, years earlier, Rene had carried off a handsome prize for French; but in camp that was of little use. There were ninety-two of us, with a house staff as diverse – Dutch, German, Czech, Welsh, Irish, along with a young English House-mother. I found myself shouldering responsibilities as Camp Commandant, with Rene as Music Mistress, and the letter-writer of this morning – the young, energetic Quaker of our company – as Keep-fit Mistress. We two New Zealanders, I remember, looked a little shyly at her, but not until today did I learn that she felt even more in doubt about us. This came in the very first letter of hers to me after hearing of Rene's death. She had always addressed my friend as "Watty" – with her permission – since that first hour together, when she learnt that Rene's family name was "Watts". Our warm-hearted friendship has grown.

Her letter started with the words: "What a lovely person she was!" Spanning the rich years our friend, then unmarried, is now a widow, with a young son at her side, and she gave her kind permission for me to quote from her letter: "I haven't written often," said she, "but I've had you much in mind lately – thinking back to our camp days; and to times when you have been able to stay here briefly. There was one time, I remember, when you had soon to go on with your publisher's itinerary; but 'Watty' could stay a little longer – and we liked that.

"I feel sure I've never told you, after our introduction there at camp, how doubtful I had felt about working with two as 'close' as you were. But you soon taught me that 'exclusiveness' was not in your vocabulary. In fact, you showed me how two females could live together, and not in each other's pockets – each with a full life of service of her own. No one knows as well as I", she added, "the gap her going leaves in your life. (Let me know when your book with its special last chapter on 'Watty' comes out – and what its title is – I must have that.) [Note: it is *Continually Aware*.]

"When she was staying here at that time – you may not know it – she planted some crocuses in my garden. And now we have a carpet of them, and we always look for the first of 'Watty's' crocuses to come out."

No, I didn't know of them – it was one of those very natural things Rene did, without speaking about it. And now it's her "memorial", Spring by Spring, in the garden, and in the heart of our friend. I was so moved to hear of those crocuses; and I can't think of any more suitable memorial – so beautiful and hopeful!

This morning before the mail came – working on this book – I had been for some time reading and studying Mark's fourteenth chapter. It recorded the nameless woman in Bethany, who expressed her love in a beautiful, special way, and in the last verse of Mark's record of it, he gives us the Master's commendation, translated into our word "memorial" (Mark 14:3-9). This is the only time that the word appears anywhere in Mark's writings.

I had started to draw attention to it in Mark's gospel,

where it fittingly belongs, when our Quaker friend's letter came. I had already taken down my *Concise Oxford Dictionary*, to see what it had to say under the word "Memorial", and had just read, by way of definition, the words "status, festival, serving to commemorate; of memory; custom, etc; record, chronicle, etc." But there I find no mention of "crocuses", though for me they will always now be associated with what season by season our eyes may see, and our spirits remember. I once before wrote of some crocuses that Rene had gathered from our own garden and set upon my desk – gloriously golden like the sun, always a miracle, as if a measure of hopefulness was shining through them.

Wordsworth spoke of his heart leaping up when he beheld a rainbow in the sky; so my heart leaps up when I behold a crocus in the earth. Old Gerard, in his *Herball*, at the end of the sixteenth century, described them as "Floures of a perfect shining yellow colour, seeming afar off to be a hot glowing coal of fire."

One morning early in England, speechlessness laid hold of me when I came upon what I had lately seen as a fresh green sward, now covered with crocuses beside the river in Cambridge! It was a chill, crisp morning – so that I was glad of woolly gloves and scarf – but there were the crocuses spelling out a lively hope! Old Hanbury, succeeding Gerard at the end of the eighteenth century, made an attempt to describe them. "They are all of them", he said, "very beautiful" – to which I would add "and very hopeful." I understand Parson Sydney Smith's exclamation as he came on a crocus lifting its head above the early snow: "The Resurrection! The Resurrection!" And in our day Canon Sinker is as ecstatic: "Crocuses", he says, "seem to greet God with the 'Hallelujah Chorus' ! "

Snow can intimidate us; but crocuses do not wait till everything is propitious. That, it seems, is why translators of the Revised Standard Version of the Bible render a well-known passage in Isaiah: "The wilderness and the dry land shall be glad, the desert shall rejoice and blossom; like the crocus it shall blossom abundantly" (Isaiah 35:1-2). Knowing how reluctant some people would be to lose "the rose" of the familiar Authorized Version for "the crocus", a little note has been added to justify this change. It is not only a change agreed on by the scholars; but one wholly in keeping with all that we know of courage and hopefulness!

"We need more crocuses among humans," said Dr Halford Lucock, late Professor of Preaching at Yale Divinity School, "people who take the first possible – or impossible – chance at getting something worthwhile done. The world has moved forward on the ventures of crocus-minded people. When the Apostle Paul sailed across the narrow sea from Asia to Europe," our ever-hopeful doctor delighted to remind us, "there was to human view not a chance that he would ever make a dent on Europe with the story of a condemned criminal executed in Palestine." Yet he did – and so the Gospel of the Crucified, Risen Christ came to Europe, and in the process of time, to us. It was a courageous and hopeful undertaking. "Paul was a crocus, pushing up in the dead of winter."

And there are any number of characters of whom we can read today, in available autobiography and biography, who have laid hold of this same secret. These are the men and women of our time who make it possible for the Church of the Living Christ to witness in the world. And they are not all of one skin colour, language or denomination. They are crocus-minded characters who follow in His way, in thought, worship and service.

You may know the lovely Authorized Version of the story of Mark preserved for succeeding generations, in his little gospel, but in case you don't have it all off by heart, let me copy its meaning here, by way of refreshing your memory. It turns on an unforgettable set of values that, realized in day to day relationships for Love's sake, are everlasting. Our Master used the word which is translated for us in our New Testament as "memorial".

"In Greek", as Dr William Barclay rejoiced to remind us, "there are two words for good – there is *agathos* which describes a thing which is *morally good*. And there is *kalos* which describes a thing which is *not only good but lovely*." The woman's gift to Christ, which was her memorial, was of this latter kind!

* * *

Here is Mark's rendering of it: "After two days was the feast of the passover, and of unleavened bread: and the chief priests and the scribes sought how they might take Him by craft, and put Him to death. But they said, Not on the feast day, lest there be an uproar of the people.

"And being in Bethany in the house of Simon the leper, as He sat at meat, there came a woman having an alabaster box of ointment of spikenard very precious; and she brake the box, and poured it on His head. And there were some that had indignation within themselves, and said, Why was this waste of the ointment made? For it might have been sold for more than three hundred pence, and have been given to the poor. And they murmured against her. And Jesus said, Let her alone: why trouble ye her? she hath wrought a good work on Me. For ye have the poor with you always, and whensoever ye will ye may do them good: but Me ye have not always. She hath done what she could: she is come aforehand to anoint My body to the burying.

"Verily I say unto you, Wheresoever this gospel shall be preached throughout the whole world, this also that she hath done shall be spoken of *for a memorial of her*" (Mark 14:1-9).

* * *

A memorial can by anything – *but preferably something hopeful, beautiful, and self-giving*!

Travelling Light

All my life I've been a traveller, and I am still. A lot of my travelling has been done on my own two feet – in my earliest days, with a stick in one hand, and an apple in my pocket. Then when later I found myself in Britain with a pound or two as each week greeted me, I discovered I could travel from place to place with the blessing of the Youth Hostel Association. It was Springtime – the sixteenth of April, to be exact, or as the old records would have put it more beautifully, "XVIth daye of Aprylle." Turning away from buses, trains and cars, it became possible to stay at a hostel for a shilling a night – which was *twenty* "sleeps" for a pound! Two pence more provided firing – peat or wood on the hearth, gas, or an electric point – and one might thankfully boil a kettle, or cook a modest meal. I could carry all I needed in my haversack and hardly notice its weight – a change of garments, a comfortable cardigan lest the weather deteriorate, a torch, a storm-cape, spare woollen stockings, wash-things, and the inevitable plate, cup, knife, spoon and fork. Once on the way, a modest lunch could be eaten under a shady hedge.

One was also wise to squeeze in a small first aid pack – the sunniest day, with the loveliest landscape, can be lost on a traveller with a blistered heel. One very human story of St Clement, who must have done a great deal of walking, tells of at least one occasion when his feet became sore. Gathering up odd wisps of lambs' wool for the insides of his sandals, it is claimed, he discovered the useful substance of felt, as the wool matted together, a useful find for the rest of humanity.

There are always suffering feet, and there is always the

way when one must face a test between lunch and tea-time, especially when there is a long, stiffish climb. Then a song helps. Or it may be that some other hardship must be met. An early manuscript, written shortly after Chaucer's death, brings forward a lively suggestion: "I say to thee, that it is well done that Pilgrims have with them singers and also pipers, that when one of them, that goeth bare-foot, striketh his toe upon a stone, and hurteth him sore, and maketh him to bleed; it is well done that he or his fellow begin then a song, or else take out of his bosom a pipe for to drive away with such mirth the hurt of his fellow." (Did the early disciples have such problems?)

Thinking of my own habit of tossing in a few handy aids for cuts, bites and blistered heels, I find myself turning with great interest to what Mark tells us of the disciples of Jesus first setting off. They had to walk – and the roads and footpaths were everywhere then very rough. Mark says of Jesus: "He called unto Him the twelve, and began to send them forth two by two; and gave them power over unclean spirits; and commanded them that they should take nothing for their journey, save a staff only; no scrip, no bread, no money in their purse: but be shod with sandals; and not put on two coats" (Mark 6:7-9).

As Dr Alec Vidler reminds us in his little study-book on Mark's Gospel (*Read, Mark, Learn*) "These instructions vary in the different Gospels" (Matthew 9:35-10:42 and Luke 9:1-6, 10:1-16). "No doubt", Dr Vidler continues, "account was taken of the fact that what was feasible in Palestine was not so elsewhere. These are not to be regarded – nor were they from the first literally regarded – as timeless laws for missionary activity, though in many respects they have an enduring point, e.g. travelling light and not fussing about superfluous accessories." "What counts", he quotes another scholar,

Rudolf Schnackenburg, as saying in *The Gospel according to St Mark* (Sheed and Ward), "is the spirit of apostolic simplicity." They were to travel light, and to accept the hospitality that people offered them.

In the easily understood language of our day Dr Halford Luccock says in *The Interpreter's Bible*, "The main thing is to get on with the work. Do not get bogged down with a burdensome sense of responsibility for paraphernalia. No bread, no bag, no money, the simplest clothes. Travel light, so that the work may get the whole of your undivided mind and soul. The emphasis", he adds, "has a pertinence for all time."

I think so!

* * *

Many more of us are travelling these days – so that this Christian message about "travelling light" should come clearly to us. When our grandmothers and great-grand-mothers travelled, luggage was a terrible trial. Immense brass-bound trunks, stuffed tight, were the possession of almost all who came to my home country in its early days. And for the next generation or two, ships, coaches and trains had all to travel long distances, chock-a-block with heavy, awkward luggage. My own aunts and uncles all inherited these great travelling pieces in the next generation – when full they were far too heavy to lift without help from neighbouring men; when empty, they took up far more room than could be spared in the front hall, or at the top of the stairs, reducing play space for children on wet days.

Of course, grandparents and great-grandparents had come a long way in a sailing ship, with small expectation of ever returning to the old land that gave them birth. As far as they were concerned, it meant for many the break up of the old family home, and the sharing of possessions long treasured there. Trinkets, pictures and pieces of furniture were suddenly theirs, work boxes, music boxes and countless books. And, of course, there was no way of learning what could be had in the new country, so it was wise to take with you the things that had come to be counted necessary in life. Clothes then too, of course, were thick and clumsy to pack.

Years on, some of those daring early travellers did return to see relations left in the old country, some never did. It was as much as they could do to travel by cart or lumbering coach to see their young people, grown up with the passing years, married and settled a hundred or less miles away. One lady described herself as travelling, anxiously mulling over her inventory, "Big box, little box, hand-box, bundle".

Even looking back to my own first world journey, that became possible in my early twenties, as one born in the country, on that first voyage I took with me a cabin-trunk – but never again. Setting off, a dear friend's parting gift – supported by much advice – was one of the little new electric irons, a modern marvel not available when she had made her own solo trip. But by that time, I had written a book and was to be received by publishers who were arranging a modest lecture itinerary for me. This, of course, was well before the light, handy, nylon, drip-dry age. Nothing out of my luggage could be worn at a ship's party, or even a simple game of bowls on deck, without first being pressed by the ship's iron, in a limited ironing room below deck. In the Tropics that would be a hot trial. But in time I would part with even that convenience, and once ashore would have to depend on my little iron when meeting publishers or standing on a public platform. I might enjoy some confidence of being uncrushed, as my good friend planned, through her little iron. But the iron and I became a great trial to each other. Apart from its weight, there was always the possibility that I would throw a hotel here and there into complete darkness, and myself out into the street, by reason of the difference between "direct" and "indirect" current fed into it. It was always an additional anxiety, except when I was staying in private homes, which I welcomed in the struggle to be "uncrushed". Nobody could have been kinder to me, as I travelled from place to place, from pulpit to platform, than family friends and publishers. In one family there was happily a teenage daughter, soon to set up a shared flat with a business friend in a city a distance from home. I have never yet actually been there, but it was occasion enough for me to contribute a "handy gift" – and a very unexpected one – to that new flat! And from that moment, unlike Lot's wife in the early Bible story, I never looked back.

Soon, I was travelling by plane, and learning some other secrets of "travelling light". Mindful of airline officers ahead of me waiting to charge for overweight luggage, I have several times been known to cut a new cake of bathsoap in half, before setting out!

* * *

The Latin for baggage, I am told, is *impedimenta* – a word that in itself seems overweight and clumsy to me, as one of this earth's light travellers. "*It is pleasant*", said that great modern day traveller, Freya Stark, who has shared so much with me through her writings, "*now and then to go among people who carry their lives lightly.*"

That is a saying to value, as we come towards the close of this chapter with its responsible title, for as Mark well knew, when he set down what the Master said about "travelling light", it was at heart a spiritual matter. Staffs, sandals, coats were symbolic of "things" in this life, set to serve or be cast aside – even good things could not be allowed to dominate, and become impedimenta. It is so easy, we find, to let them take charge.

Very sad as well, remains our travelling habit of carrying in our spirits, loads of less worthy human hates, slights, resentments, fears, grudges, and angular, awkward chunks of pride.

*　　*　　*

And this secret of course is not alone for individual disciples – it's an issue, as Dr Nathaniel Micklem was concerned to say, "that moves out from the centre, to its communal application. If the Christian in his own life must travel light, so the Church, facing the new world that is coming into being, must travel light", being willing to leave behind much accumulated to no spiritual purpose!

Is Being Good Any Good?

If you have ever pushed a pram up the street with a baby in it – your own, or somebody else's – you will remember the question asked you at almost every stop, as mother, auntie or neighbour – "Is he good?"

There was no one to ask God the Creator a like question when He made the world – "Is it good?" Happily, He knew the answer – and it was important to Him. The opening verses of the Bible leave us in no doubt: "In the beginning God created the heaven and the earth. And the earth was without form, and void; and darkness was upon the face of the deep. And the Spirit of God moved upon the face of the waters. And God said, Let there be light: and there was light. And God saw the light, *that it was good*" (Genesis 1:1-4).

That was a wonderful beginning!

And then came the creation of the firmament – "And God called the firmament Heaven. And the evening and the morning were the second day. And God said, Let the waters under the heaven be gathered together unto one place, and let the dry land appear: and it was so. And God called the dry land Earth; and the gathering together of the waters called He Seas; *and God saw that it was good*". (Genesis 1:8-10).

And God said, Let there be lights in the firmament of the heaven to . . . give light upon the earth: and it was so. And God made two great lights; the greater light to rule the day, and the lesser light to rule the night: He made the stars also. And God set them in the firmament of the heaven to give light upon the earth, and to rule over the day and over the night, and to divide the light from the darkness: *and God saw that it was good.* And the evening and the morning were the fourth day . . . " (1:14-19).

And on goes the furnishing of the earth with beast and cattle after its own kind, after the waters and the skies have been blessed with suitable living creatures. "And God made the beast of the earth after his kind, and cattle after their kind, and every thing that creepeth upon the earth after his kind; *and God saw that it was good*" (1:25).

And at this point came the peopling of the world with man and woman – with dominion over the creatures granted to their care. And so the first wonderful chapter leads us on to the seventh day – the Creator's day of rest.

But with the rich gift of human choice, it was never again so easy to count on things being wholly good, day after day , but God felt it important to take that risk. He had set His heart on a relationship of Love – and we earth people must be left to choose; Love cannot be forced!

But goodness is of more than one kind, different from the good baby in his pram, sleeping well, facing what each day brings without bawling his head off. There is the little child – little boy, little girl – being sent off for the day on a visit to Nanna, to Auntie. The parting word hardly varies at all: "Now be good, won't you!" Meaning, eat up what is offered you; don't make an unwelcome noise; or get your clothes dirty! That is a slightly higher kind of good, because there is a measure of human choice there.

And that is something more we have to learn – as our birthdays mount up, and we can be referred to, behind our backs, as "a good boy", "a good girl", meaning that we don't step out of our night attire in the morning, leaving it in a muddle on the floor; we keep our bags and schoolbooks tidy, where we can lay hands on them each morning without causing a commotion; we do our homework without too much urging; we lend a hand with the dishes; run a message cheerfully and promptly when asked; and remember with a small gift and a suitable word other people's birthdays, as well as our own; don't forget to say "thank you" when a gift arrives, or something pleases us!

Nor is this matter at an end yet, if we are to have a "good part" in this world that God made and called "good", and in which He set us to rejoice and share. Trouble starts when what is called "good" in the home, in outside companionship, in one's first job, earns that recognition only when it is quiet, biddable, no-trouble-to-anyone. That is all too likely to be negative and dull – and at home, at work, and at church that is disastrous, especially in one's experience of church, and all the ramifications of religion.

I've always liked the way Katherine Mansfield, our longtime New Zealand story writer put it, in seeking to sum up the day to day manifestation of religion: It was, she was persuaded, "to make the commonplace virtues as attractive as the ordinary vices. To present the good as the witty, the adventurous, the romantic, the gay, the alluring, and the evil as the dull, the solemn, the conventional, and the unattractive."

"I would rather be bad than a 'goody–goody' ", says a disadvantaged, though honest youngster in Harold Loukes' present-day book, *Teenage Religion* (S.C.M. Press). "It is boring to be too good", says another. It makes sorry reading; for neither will lay hold of life's real adventure until he discovers that *there's a world of difference between being "good" and being "goody-goody"*. I wish that these two, and others who speak like them, could happen upon a man like Dr Edward Wilson, who went south to the Antarctic with Captain Scott. There was nothing "goody-goody" about him – a doctor, an artist, a young husband, a valiant companion, "Bill" to his mates. George Seaver wrote his biography after his all too early death, and Apsley Cherry-Garrard, who knew him well, wrote a stirring introduction to the book, beginning it with: "If this book succeeds in showing what kind of man Bill was, it will give you courage . . . You will read here the story of a man who, however appalling the conditions, and whatever the dangers . . . just went on doing his job . . . You must not think of Bill as a 'religious man'. [He means "religious" in the worst sense, as "goody-goody" or "dull".] . . . it is literal truth that this was a happy expedition."

No one ever said of his Divine Master that He was "goody-goody" or dull; much less that He required His modern-day servant to be either. It was from the start the Pharisees and like leaders who, by contrast, were dull, droning out their prayers, standing in the market place, multiplying pettyfogging laws and regulations to lay a heavy weight upon the spirit. Jesus was not like that. How could such things be said of Jesus? His first public engagement was a wedding feast, an occasion of family joy.

And how naturally, on that other occasion, He made friends with little children! Mark found room to record that as an important characteristic. To him, it was good! (Mark 10:13-15). Plainly the children showed no fear of Him; His adult presence in no way froze the smiles on their lips. They knew a winsomeness that was His, despite the efforts of the disciples to send them away in order to save His time and energies for more important duties.

Setting a modern Christian woman beside the witness of Dr Edward Wilson, a man whose actions were so strong and inspiring, I like the telling witness in words that Dorothy Sayers summoned to speak of religion as she knew it. Blessed with a longtime ability to read her New Testament in Greek, she rejoiced to pass on the strong inspiration of Mark's gospel and those that were written later. From her rich findings, she not only strengthened her own faith but gave us, as well as her many books, her wonderful drama *The Man Born To Be King*, both in book form, and as broadcast by the B.B.C. It is impossible to tell how many millions of us stood up a little straighter in our Christian witness, because of it! There was nothing "goody-goody" or "dull" about that glorious Message, nor the manner of its sharing. Of the basic story of Jesus which gives us our religion to this day Dorothy Sayers wrote unforgettably: "If this is dull, then what, in Heaven's name, is worthy to be called exciting? The people who hanged Christ never, to do them justice, accused Him of being a bore – on the contrary, they thought Him too dynamic to be safe." Of the redeeming Gospel that He brought to this world she says rightly, "It is a tragedy to neglect it, and a crime to make it dull!"

I pray, even more eagerly as I grow older – with a little petition added: "*And let my goodness be gracious.*" Religion at its source is an adventure in living, and for ever!

A Donkey Can Serve!

In Jerusalem is a biblical zoo, in which, thanks to Professor Aharon Shulov of the Hebrew University, are gathered representatives of the creatures that had a part in the life of our Lord. Were it possible, how pleased Mark would be to know this, keeping them all in mind – the donkey, the cow, the sheep, among others, with the donkey leading.

For that humble animal had an important place in our Lord's life that Mark gloried in! And on several occasions.

I must say I was glad when I came across a little poem lately, by some unknown writer, putting the donkey first – the cow and sheep following:

> "I", said the donkey, shaggy and brown,
> "I carried His mother up hill and down,
> I carried her safely to Bethlehem Town,
> I", said the donkey, shaggy and brown.
>
> "I", said the cow, all white and red,
> "I gave Him my manger for His bed,
> I gave Him my hay to pillow His head,
> I", said the cow all white and red.
>
> "I", said the sheep with curly horn,
> "I gave Him my wool to keep Him warm,
> I gave Him my coat on Christmas morn,
> I", said the sheep with the curly horn.

It has been one of the great pleasures of my life to witness a Royal Coronation procession, taking up my appointed seat on the roadside between Buckingham Palace and

Westminster. But this procession of which Mark rejoiced to tell was different – a Royal procession surely, but different. There were no royal carriages, no high-stepping horses; no crowds assembled from the ends of the earth; no bunting displayed along the route to be travelled – only a Man astride a young donkey that had never before done service of the kind that day required of him.

He was purposefully chosen well beforehand, as part of the essential preparation. Any procession needs such planning if it is to go without a hitch on the day, whether it be in London, where it took months and months to make ready, or in Jerusalem, the Holy City. There it was a simpler matter, but important that a young donkey should be available, rather than a horse. In Palestine, any king riding to war, or at any other time if he wished to declare himself a conqueror, rode a horse; it was only if his purpose was one of peace, that he rode a donkey. As Jesus made His way into Jerusalem, the city He loved, He meant thus to declare in a dramatic way that He was the Messiah – and coming in peace. In the minds of many of the people would be the famous saying of the prophet Zechariah: "Rejoice greatly, O daughter of Zion; shout, O daughter of Jerusalem: behold, thy King cometh unto thee: he is just, and having salvation; lowly, and riding upon an ass, and upon a colt the foal of an ass" (Zechariah 9:9).

Jesus, of course, had entered Jerusalem a number of times, first as a lad of twelve, when He accompanied His earth-parents, Mary and Joseph. But this was different – Mark leaves his readers in no doubt about that. "And when they came nigh to Jerusalem . . . at the Mount of Olives, He sendeth forth two of His disciples, and saith unto them, Go your way into the village over against you: and as soon as ye be entered into it, ye shall find a colt tied, whereon never man sat; loose him, and bring him. And if any man saith unto you, Why do ye this? say ye that the Lord hath need of him; and straightway he will send him hither!

"And they went their way, and found the colt tied by the door without in a place where two ways met; and they loose him. And certain of them that stood there said unto them, What do ye, loosing the colt? And they said unto them even as Jesus had commanded: and they let them go. And they brought the colt to Jesus, and cast their garments on him; and He sat upon him.

"And many spread their garments in the way: and others cut down branches off the trees, and strewed them in the way. And they that went before, and they that followed, cried, saying, Hosanna, Blessed is He that cometh in the name of the Lord: blessed be the kingdom of our father David, that cometh in the name of the Lord: Hosanna in the highest.

"And Jesus entered into Jerusalem, and into the temple: and when He had looked round about upon all things, and now the eventide was come, He went out unto Bethany with the twelve" (Mark 11:1-11).

So, the little donkey was used of Jesus, and there, in that procession, met His need. My friend Dr Leonard Small, until recently serving at St Cuthbert's, in Edinburgh, and travelling the wide world, found himself grateful to Mark for focusing attention on the use of a common donkey, and preached about it very tellingly, finding a place for it in his book *No Uncertain Sound*. And as we talked together lately over a meal, he kindly gave me permission to quote his words. "Palm Sunday", he says, "sets before every one of us the challenging and inspiring thought that Jesus Christ needs us . . . Without that peculiar contribution that is mine alone to make, His plan miscarries if what He asks and needs of me is withheld, then something is missing." (This is longer than most quotes from another friend whose words I like to use, but it is so in accord with the practical spirit of the situation as Mark records it, that I cannot pass it by.) "This pattern", says Dr Small, "runs all through the gospels. Constantly we see Jesus needing something which men can give, and realize that by asking for it He binds them to Himself. He needs a place to be born when He comes down to earth from heaven, being truly made bone of our bone and flesh of our flesh. He finds one tiny corner of caring and compassion and response in the heart of a busy, bothered innkeeper who has no room . . . but who gives a stable, a place at least of warmth, and privacy, with a pile of straw for a birth-place and a manger for a crib, and – Lo and behold! – what God has planned actually works out.

"He is preaching to the crowd at the side of the Sea of Galilee, and they press upon Him almost to the water's edge. He asks Peter to pull on the mooring rope of his fishing boat, floating quietly just off shore; He climbs on board, gets Peter to push her off again and uses the bow of the boat as a pulpit. Was that when He first began to lay hold on Peter's warm but reliable heart?

"He is sitting tired in the shade by the well of Samaria. A woman comes to draw water in the heat of the day, coming then to avoid the sly glances and gossiping tongues of her fellow women. He asks her to draw water and give Him a drink, and by asking that service makes contact with her to her eternal salvation.

"He needs some food to satisfy a huge crowd, and a boy gives Him what was probably the remains of his own picnic lunch – could that boy ever forget the look that Jesus gave him?

"He needs a young donkey to fulfil the prophecy and come as a King, yet in peace. Someone has such a beast and arranges to make it available.

"He needs some tiny act of love to lift His heart, to make Him feel that He can win in the end, and Mary anoints Him at Bethany.

"On the Via Dolorosa He stumbles under the weight of His Cross; Simon is compelled, at first against his will, to bear the Cross, and then, surely, he lends his strong shoulder gladly.

"His broken body needs a tomb, and Joseph, openly loyal when it seems too late, gives it. We can see how this pattern of His needing something we can give, runs through it all."

And that is not only true, but becomes our life's most glorious reality. G.K. Chesterton imagines the little donkey that led that procession on the way into Jerusalem, refusing the pity of the crowd, for the fact that he was such a simple creature for such a service, and instead has him say –

> . . . I also had my hour,
> One far fierce hour and sweet;
> There was a shout about my ears,
> And palms about my feet!

And many a modest human "donkey" has lived to say as much, and to give praise to Christ, and thanks that he or she was needed.

A long time ago now, on the edge of my study desk, where I offer daily what I have to give, I set what I call my "donkey prayer", fashioned from words of Thomas à Kempis:

> Lord, in the simplicity of my heart,
> I offer myself to Thee today,
> to be Thy servant for ever . . .

And beside it, for when the new day finds me in the mood to sing, I have set my "donkey hymn":

> Wherever in the world I am,
>   In whatsoever estate,
> I have a fellowship with hearts
>   To keep and cultivate,

A Donkey Can Serve!

And a work of lowly love to do
   For the Lord on Whom I wait.

I ask Thee for the daily strength
   To none that ask denied,
And a mind to blend with outward
     life,
   Still keeping at Thy side,
Content to fill a little space
   If Thou be glorified.

(From *The Methodist Hymn Book,*
               602)

Bread and Wine

Whilst Mark was growing up into young manhood, there can have been in Jerusalem no sizeable building with an upper room more significant than Mark's own home.

And one season, Jesus and his disciples found their feet wending in that direction. Jesus was not one to leave things to the last moment. Well before, He must have reached an understanding with Mark's mother, who was known to be a generous soul.

Before Jesus had arranged to pick up a young animal on which He would ride into Jerusalem, He must have known that His disciples would come asking where they could prepare to eat the Passover, and He had arranged that they should look out for "a man carrying an earthen pitcher of water". This was clearly a pre-arranged signal, for to carry a water-pot was a woman's duty. It was a thing that no man would ever normally do.

The large room they would occupy was to be approached from an outside stair. This type of room had a number of uses – sometimes as a store-room; sometimes as a place for quiet and meditation; or as a place where a Rabbi taught his chosen band of intimate disciples; or as a guest room when visitors arrived unexpectedly.

To this, we read, "His disciples went forth, and came into the city, and found as He had said unto them: and they made ready the Passover. And in the evening He cometh with the Twelve.

"And as they sat and did eat, Jesus said, Verily I say unto you, one of you which eateth with Me shall betray Me. And they began to be sorrowful, and to say unto him one by one, Is it I? and another said, Is it I? And He answered and said unto them, It is one of the twelve, that dippeth with Me in the dish. The Son of Man indeed goeth, as it is written of Him: but woe to that man by whom the Son of Man is betrayed! good were it for that man if he had never been born.

["Mark", says Dr Alec Vidler, in *Read, Mark, Learn*, "is concerned to show that Jesus was not taken by surprise by the treachery of Judas."]

"And as they did eat," adds Mark, "Jesus took bread, and blessed, and brake it, and gave to them, and said, Take, eat: this is My body. And He took the cup, and when He had given thanks, He gave it to them: and they all drank of it. And He said unto them, This is My blood of the new testament, which is shed for many" (Mark 14:16-24).

This last meal together was being held at the Passover time, just before the death of Jesus, but it was clearly much more than that to Him, and to them! "The Passover", as Dr David Cairns reminds us, in his study *In Remembrance of Me*, was held at that holy time, an annual festival to gather the families of Israel together to commemorate their forebears' deliverance long, long before in Egypt." But this Supper in itself was quite different. "Jesus", he says, "claimed that by this death of His which was to come so soon, God would inaugurate the New Covenant which He was about to make with His people" (p.29).

And then, to those of us reading this little book I am sharing with you, he says: "And we must further note, from the gospel of Mark, the wideness and generosity of this offer, for Jesus said, '*This is My blood of the covenant, shed for many*' (Mark 14:24; N.E.B.).

"The Passover was an occasion of solemn remembrance, thanksgiving and joy. Though celebrated by families in their homes and not in the Temple, it was also a national feast. All those who were able, came to Jerusalem, and the city was full of visitors.

"A solemn ritual was observed at the feast, and it

probably varied but little. One man in each household acted as the President, most commonly the father of the family. It was usual for men, women and children to share in it, but it was also possible for a group of men, like Jesus and His disciples, to sit down together.''

But this Last Supper in the Upper Room was clearly something different. Those who took part in it were closely associated with the Master of the meal. They were soon to experience the loss of His visible, physical presence. Commenting on it, Professor D.M. Baillie, the distinguished Scottish theologian of our day, said simply: "I'm sure His disciples didn't understand half of what it meant. But after He was gone, it came back to them, and they began to do it over again in His name. And whenever they did it, they felt and knew that after all, Christ was not far away from them. Sometimes in their endeavour to live the Christian life they would grow weary and doubtful and dimsighted, just as we do. Jesus seemed but a distant memory, an unreal shadow. But then they would come together, and do this simple thing. And the reality of Christ came back to them again. He became known unto them, as Acts 2:42 says 'and they continued stedfastly in the apostles' doctrine and fellowship, and in breaking of bread, and in prayers'.''

It was a beautiful meaningful thing that He gave them – and us – to do in this Service of Bread and Wine, carrying a share of the Love of our Lord who receives us at His table, making everlastingly real to us the sense of His living nearness.

It has long been the custom between dear friends to exchange a gift at parting – a picture, a ring, or some other treasured thing – but Jesus had nothing of this sort. Even if he had possessed such a token in all the strange and scattered adventures of the years they might have lost it, or they might have squabbled over it as men have done over relics, or they might even have worshipped it. *But He gave them instead something to do*. And He showed them, before He went out from that Upper Room that Mark knew well, how it might be done. It was something that those who followed Him, both men and women, those who loved Him, *could do anywhere*, even the very poorest could do it. And down the centuries since, men and women, "in remembrance of Him", have kept this feast in "upper rooms"; in times of danger; in the catacombs; like the Covenanters, up in the glens; in modest meeting houses; and in hospitals, homes and churches, as diverse as those in which we find ourselves Sunday by Sunday.

It does not greatly matter what we call this simple feast – each title tells us something of its meaning.

I have many times, the world round, shared this hallowed service passed down to us from that never-to-be-forgotten night of Communion in the Upper Room of Mark's home. (He himself was not present, but his friend, Peter, was there and he told Mark of that happening (Mark 14:12-26).) Humbly, in my turn, I have broken the bread and shared the wine outpoured, on shipboard in the mighty Atlantic, and in a modest Mission Chapel, roofed with palm-leaves in the Pacific; in Bavaria, and yet again in a great cathedral in Denmark. Nor will I forget, what a poet friend of mine called "Communion in the Prison Yard". (The men of whom he wrote were two of a limited number who had taken up the pacifist position during the War.)

No hallowed aisles have we to worship in;
No silver chalice brimmed with mystic wine;
Save for our carolling hearts we have no choir,
No vestments but the peasant clothes we wear.
Yet faith has set her table of poor timber
For the chief Guest; adoring, we remember
Our Lord has broken the scraps of bread we bless
And round us shines the cloud of witnesses.
Since He is risen, Love makes light of walls,

And in this desert yard spring up sweet wells
Of pardoning peace. We drink deep and are glad
With a most solemn gladness, seeing His thirst, His
    head
Heavy with death for us; as each one kneels
His grace rains down from penal thorns and nails.

Basil Dowling

Ageless Words

A steeply descending, ankle-shocking pathway leads one today down from the Mount of Olives, to pause a moment reverently at the point where Jesus wept over the city, where now a small church stands, *Dominus Flevit*.

Another break in that stumbling walk – for ever meaningful – is at the wall, where a gate gives way into "The Garden of Gethsemane", with its ancient olives. This is, indeed, holy ground! And here we remember what must have been Jesus' most precious Aramaic words "*Abba*, Father!" It was the simple term of approach used by a small trusting Jewish child, in coming into the fellowship of his father. And here, Jesus used these words in prayer – as He bowed in the holy presence of God His Father. In his little book, Mark wrote: "And He taketh with Him Peter and James and John, and began to be sore amazed, and to be very heavy; and saith unto them, My soul is exceeding sorrowful unto death: tarry ye here, and watch. And He went forward a little, and fell on the ground, and prayed that, if it were possible, the hour might pass from Him. And He said, *Abba*, Father, all things are possible unto Thee; take away this cup from Me: nevertheless not what I will, but what Thou wilt.

"And He cometh, and findeth them sleeping, and saith unto Peter, Simon, sleepest thou? couldest thou not watch one hour? Watch ye and pray, lest ye enter into temptation. The spirit truly is ready, but the flesh is weak. And again He went away, and prayed, and spake the same words. And when He returned, He found them asleep again (for their eyes were heavy), neither wist they what to answer Him. And He cometh the third time, and saith unto them, Sleep on now, and take your rest: it is enough, the hour is come; behold the Son of Man is betrayed into the hands of sinners. Rise up, let us go; lo, he that betrayeth Me is at hand.

"And immediately, while He yet spake, cometh Judas, one of the twelve, and with him a great multitude with swords and staves, from the chief priests and the scribes and the elders. And he that betrayed Him had given them a token, saying, Whomsoever I shall kiss, that same is He; take Him, and lead Him away safely. And as soon as he was come, he goeth straightway to Him, and saith, Master, master; and kissed Him.

"And they laid their hands on Him, and took Him" (Mark 14:32-46).

* * *

I shall remember always that, as I walked down that way to the gate that led into Gethsemane, there flowered at that moment, on the wall, a passion-flower, with a cross at its heart!

And I recalled, as I entered and was led forward by a gentle old "brother", in the simple habit of his order, some words from Dr Gibb, that I had tried to memorize: "Communion with God is itself a form of prayer, but unless we take heed, the communion may easily degenerate into a dreamy, misty abstraction . . . Real prayer is hard toil, and knowledge of God is never to be gained without sweat." Writing of *The Fellowship of His Sufferings*, in my book of devotions, *While The Candle Burns* (Epworth Press, 1942), I had used those words. But standing within the shade of the present-day eight old olive trees there, and beside the little garden patch beneath, tended by the old "brother", moving gently with his hoe, they seemed to carry a more tremendous meaning.

* * *

I had succeeded in memorizing a poem I'd come upon in my teens, written by a Christian, Sidney Lanier (between 1842 and 1881). But now it did not go as far, or as deeply, as Mark's own words. Lanier had written, in what he called "A Ballad of Trees and The Master":

> Into the woods my Master went,
> Clean forespent, forespent.
> Into the woods my Master came,
> Forespent with love and shame.
> But the Olives they were not blind to Him;
> The little gray leaves were kind to Him;
> When into the woods He came.
>
> Out of the woods my Master went,
> And He was well content.
> Out of the woods my Master came,
> Content with Death and shame.
> When Death and shame would woo Him fast,
> From under the trees they drew Him last;
> 'Twas on a tree they slew Him – last
> When out of the woods He came.

*   *   *

All too soon the judgement, and His Cross followed. We cannot worthily comment on that terrible cry, in His own Aramaic words: "*Eloi, Eloi, lama, sabachthani*?", which is, being interpreted, "My God, my God, why hast Thou forsaken Me?" (Mark 15:34).

And Mary, His mother, was there, with how much more thereafter to keep in the secret places of her heart! And her Son commended her into the dear, loving care of His close friend, John, the disciple.

Under the Wide Sky

Did Mark find it painful to set down what he knew of the erection of Crosses Three under the wide sky? I feel sure he did. The other and later gospels give a fuller account of those grim happenings, beginning with the arrest by night in Gethsemane.

Though I have never heard Mark's record read aloud at a Good Friday Service, it is the one in which the teller identifies himself, in a way that the others do not (Mark 14:41-51). After recounting the dreadful story of Jesus in the Garden of Gethsemane returning to find his trusted friends sleeping rather than watching with him, Mark records the coming of Judas and his betrayal of Jesus to the authorities.

The painful drama was under way, and soon the disciples "all forsook Him, and fled", says verse 50, where Mark goes on to identify himself with the prisoner. "There followed Him", he says, "a certain young man, having a linen cloth cast about his naked body; and the young men laid hold on him: and he left the linen cloth, and fled from them naked" (verse 52).

The pain of identification was something that Mark would never forget – or want to forget. Nor should any one of us. That came strikingly to my consideration as I walked alone along beside the Thames and came to Berkshire's little green village of Cookham, where the widely known artist Stanley Spencer had lived. I knew that in the Tate Gallery in London hung his painting "Christ Carrying the Cross". Early on, when the men and women of the artist's village gathered to see the painting, they observed one shattering feature that nobody else had spotted. Spencer had used their own familiar faces in the crowd scenes. There they were, painted recognizably into the mob who lined the road to Calvary, who yelled, "Crucify!" The artist's biographer, Maurice Collis, later added a comment: "The King of the World passes on His way to death. What an event that He should pass through Cookham!"

And yet this is how it is, and must be, for Mark and for us each. (It must be this which makes the world famous Passion play at Oberammergau a painful experience in parts. I have never witnessed the play, because it has not yet been my fortune to be free at the proper time, but I have visited the village in an off year. There I have spoken to some who have taken part in it, and seen the actual area where it is presented to overflowing audiences; and I have talked with friends from this side of the world, who have attended.)

One privilege which came to me in Jerusalem itself, was to be invited by gentle, sensitive Franciscan monks, on a Friday mid-afternoon, to walk with them slowly, prayerfully, the way of the Via Dolorosa, along which Jesus had been made to carry His Cross. And I, a modern-day Christian, walked that route, feeling in some sense the kind of identification Mark treasured, and about which, all these years later, the people of Cookham had felt so awkward.

The fact is that the Cross of Christ did not go up on Calvary under the wide sky – companied by two thieves, on crosses each side – because men and women were then more evil than ever we show ourselves to be. As a sensitive friend, now "gone upon his way", Dr W.R. Maltby, Principal of Ilkley Methodist Deaconess College, Yorkshire, wrote in his little book *Christ and His Cross* (p.51). "It was not", he said, "through the superlative wickedness of specially malignant men that Christ died. Those who were responsible actively or passively were fairly representative of the respectabilities. Religion the bond-slave of patriotism, patriotism corrupted by contempt, prestige defending

131

itself, inertia seldom disturbed into action, insincerity exposed – such things are part of the story of mankind, and they supplied the motives for the putting to death of Christ, under the wide sky."

We are not very different from those people of whom Mark tells so graphically, so meaningfully, so painfully.

More than that, I find myself borrowing Bishop F.R. Barry's summing up, in *Questioning Faith*, "I do not think we can hope to understand what Christianity finds in the Cross, if we isolate the death of Christ either from the life of which it was the climax or from the Resurrection and Pentecost, and continuing work of the living Christ in the Church, and through the Church in the wide world. That mistake", he sums up, "has been one of the reasons which, in the past, have led so many theories – and theorists – into a cul-de-sac."

The sins that nailed Christ to His Cross were not vague seldom seen sins, to which in our most honest moments we cannot put a name. They were more common than that, known even to us church people up through the years, who are counted "respectable people".

These are realities, as we read thoughtfully through the gospel that Mark has given us. It is in no sense a remote story – it cannot be whilst we are led to consider the Cross, and in a wonderfully short time, the stone rolled away, to be part of the Resurrection.

Deep in our hearts is loving respect for one who has been in and out of Mark's story all the way. It must have moved him to write there a last record of her faithfulness, when he had told of Joseph of Arimathaea, who brought fine linen "and took Him down" from the Cross. "*And Mary Magdalene and Mary the mother . . . beheld where He was laid*" (Mark 15:46-47).

In holy love, one writer has told, in present day verse, of that total reality.

I heard two soldiers talking
As they came down the hill –
The sombre hill of Calvary,
Bleak and black and still.
And one said, "The night is late;
These thieves take long to die."
And one said, "I am sore afraid,
And yet I know not why."

I heard two women weeping
As down the hill they came,
And one was like a broken rose,
And one was like a flame.
One said, "Men shall rue
This deed their hands have done",
And one said only through her tears,
"My Son! My Son! My Son!"

Amidst the Crowds

Out on His public ministry Jesus was continually surrounded by crowds – sometimes to honour Him, sometimes to hate Him – and in between such experiences, crowds gathered out of curiosity. We must not think of His life as simple, once He set out to serve the Kingdom. For one thing, crowds make so many different claims, and have so many moods!

As the years passed, it must have seemed to Jesus a long, long way back to the pastoral quietness surrounding His growing up.

Again and again, in the unfolding of His ministry, days and nights brought heavy demands. Mark – to name but one of the gospel writers – was at pains to make this understood; to show Him eager to seek out some solitary place for renewal, once He could shake off the crowds.

Mark's first chapter is not at an end before we read of the involvement of this sensitive Master of men. "At even," we read, "when the sun did set, they brought unto Him all that were diseased, and them that were possessed with devils. And all the city was gathered together at the door" (Mark 1:32). What a distressing word picture of the crowd that gives us! (If you have ever been amidst a milling crowd in Palestine, on a hot, breathless, dust-laden day, you will more painfully read its full meaning into what Mark has written. That, I admit, was an experience from which I was thankful to escape.

An unruly crowd anywhere can be frightening, just by being a crowd. I remember, on a hot Sunday afternoon in London, unexpectedly getting caught up in a demonstration. That it came swerving out of a side street, and was both rowdy and unexplained, only made it more ominous. There had been a hint of it in the morning news; but having just arrived in the city I had not read that. Another unexpected crowd met me weeks later in, of all places, Piccadilly, known by all uncertain visitors, of course, for its crowded pavements, not to speak of its cars in thousands, and underground trains at the same time disgorging rush-hour crowds.

Above all these, there stands out for ever in my memory constant, hot crowd experiences in Hong Kong – literally one of the most crowded places on earth! Its limited space cannot be made larger, save by bringing down to the level of adjoining land the tops of its yellow, stoney hills and dumping them into the sea. On this compact area of only eleven miles in length by two in width, crowds persist. They number three and three-quarter million people! Every time one returns, it is to fear that they have grown even more. Many of the people are poorly housed, having to grow up and make something of life, from shabby little shacks of scrap, pieces of bamboo, slats of wood, and oiled paper. No paths of approach serve such homes of the very poor, which are covered by rejected pieces of corrugated iron.

Contrasted with such pitiful shelters there are many impressive dwellings, and blocks of skyward mounting storeys owned by government, company, and Church. In the very crowded places, no more than five people are allowed to occupy a room twelve feet by ten, with children counting as halves. And still others exist on pavements, flat rooftops, and staircases. Nor is there any forgetting the thousands more crowded onto fishing boats and leaky old junks in the harbour, with bits of batten providing a means of stepping from one to another.

At one time, among these homeless people who poured in, before the influx of refugees ceased, there were countless young, homeless, jobless, and hungry people. One such was a young Chinese, Francis Yip, with whom I spent a fascinating day, on the very spot acquired by a kindly, concerned old Anglican parson, Bishop Hall. In 1954, with a little company of fourteen needy lads, Francis amongst them, he moved on to a rough hillside, and set about levelling it to build on. They had only hand-tools with which to do it, and all that was dislodged from that useless slope, was carried down and dumped to make a possible building area.

There now is a centre of Christian worship and work: "The Church of the Holy Carpenter". And leading its vigorous life, years on, I found that same young, slim man, devoted, trained, travelled, and ordained to the ministry. And "The Church of the Holy Carpenter" never closes its doors.

*　　*　　*

Mark's young Master would have fitted into each aspect of that Church's ongoing work – always surrounded by crowds. He gathered about Himself the young, the purposeless, the distressed, the discouraged. Save for their surface appearance, the difference in clothes and speech, the growing company about young Francis Yip and his helpers might well have fitted into Mark's little gospel. Mark doesn't ever use the word "crowds", but in the version that reaches us the word used is "multitudes". Only in Moffatt's rendering at first does the word "crowd" stand out, and it does so again and again! In comparison, the word "multitude" strikes our ears today less demandingly, in a more leisurely way, with less shock to body, mind and spirit, than the word "crowds". But there can't have been much difference, if any.

Moffatt's version still stands out from the page, as do now some other more recent versions such as the Revised Standard Version, the Good News Bible, etc. (Mark 3:20). In another place, we read as setting: "And *a great crowd*

followed Him and thronged about Him" (Mark 5:24;
R.S.V.). In the midst of this came the needy woman to
touch the hem of His garment, if she could but press in –
believing that even such an action would be enough to heal
her. Here was not only courage but great faith. And she
was healed!

In Mark 8:1 we go on to hear of *yet another crowd* – this
time, of four thousand, all far from home, and hungry.
Have you any experience of such a company? It could be
altogether frightening, since it would be hard to guess its
mood. But Mark shows us the Master handling it without a
hitch.

And there is yet another coming together, that Mark
calls "a large crowd". Dr Moffatt's rendering of his words
leaves us in no doubt about its mood. Mark 9:14 says
simply: "On reaching the disciples, they [the Master, and
Peter, James and John who had been up the mountain with
Him] saw *a large crowd round them*, and some scribes
arguing with them." That note of Mark's has a relevance
about it that we cannot miss – how often argument lays hold
of a crowd!

* * *

But we can only express thankfulness that Mark makes
room to record how, in the presence of Jesus, a crowd is
again and again seen to break up *to reveal an individual*.
We see it here, as in the case of the woman with the
haemorrhage. And Bartimaeus, sitting blindly begging on
the roadside fringe of a milling crowd, is another example.
"Jesus Christ", as scholar Harnack tellingly reminds us,
"was the first to bring the value of every human soul to
light." And what He did must ever count in significance!

Mark gives us another lovely reminder of this towards
the end of his gospel. Great events have taken place. The
Master, in the discharge of His accepted ministry, has set

His face "to go steadfastly up to Jerusalem". Already the shadow of the Cross is over His way. Entrusted with the Gospel of God's Grace, the choice now before Him is to be put to silence about it, or to be put to death. And He knows what His choice must be!

Soon, drawn from His prayer time in Gethsemane, He must stand in the Judgement Hall, with the Cross all too soon raised between heaven and earth. "And when they had crucified Him", says Mark, in what has come down to us as chapter 15:24, "they parted His garments, casting lots upon them, what every man should take. And it was the third hour, and they crucified Him. And the superscription of His accusation was written over, THE KING OF THE JEWS . . . And when the centurion, which stood over against Him, saw that He so cried out, and gave up the ghost, he said, Truly this man was the Son of God!

"There were also women looking on afar off . . . [who also, when He was in Galilee, followed Him, and ministered unto Him] and many other women which came up with Him unto Jerusalem."

Mark had prepared us for that, in what he had told us before his little book came suddenly to an end. He had shared the amazing message carried by the faithful women, Mary Magdalene, Mary the mother of James, and Salome, who brought their sweet spices as soon as possible to anoint His body. "And very early in the morning the first day of the week," are Mark's words, "they came unto the sepulchre at the rising of the sun. And they said among themselves, Who shall roll us away the stone from the door of the sepulchre?"

None of the other gospels record that typical woman's question, it is a detail that only Mark makes room for. Turn up the other records of how the women came that early morning to the tomb, and see how it's skipped over, even though it is very striking. Matthew 28:1-4 says: "In the end of the sabbath, as it began to dawn toward the first day of the week, came Mary Magdalene and the other Mary to see the sepulchre. And, behold, there was a great earthquake: for the angel of the Lord descended from heaven, and came and rolled back the stone from the door, and sat upon it." Luke, covering the same event, in chapter 24:1-3 says: "Now upon the first day of the week, very early in the morning, they came unto the sepulchre, bringing the spices which they had prepared, and certain others with them. And they found the stone rolled away from the sepulchre. And they entered in, and found not the body of the Lord Jesus." John, in his turn, is as forgetful of how the women felt unable to move the stone at the sepulchre – the most natural concern, I would have thought, as they drew near. His record (John 20:1) reads: "The first day of the week cometh Mary Magdalene early, when it was yet dark, unto the sepulchre, and seeth the stone taken away from the sepulchre." Not there, that natural question standing on the forefront of overwrought, grieving women's minds! Only Mark inserted that detail into his gospel, and it makes me feel at one with those women that morning.

It leaves me wondering whether Mark could have told me more about the amazing changes in the personalities of those followers of Jesus – so very human, in many ways, that we even find them arguing as to who should be counted greatest among them, whilst their Lord, bearing a heavier load than His mind and Spirit had ever known, was actually on His way to the Cross. But Mark did underline the great secret of the change in those frail, human men. They must have looked a bit scared, as they faced a being in "a long white garment" as they entered into the sepulchre; for the first words he spoke to them were: "Be not affrightened" (Mark 16:6). And then He had time to say unto them, the most wonderful thing of all: "Ye seek Jesus of Nazareth, which was crucified: He is risen; He is not here: behold the place where they laid Him. But go your way, tell His disciples and Peter. '' That's a nice touch, that only Mark adds, but he does so, knowing Peter's impulsiveness, and his moment of greatness later.

Faithful Hearts

It is a joy every time we read of it, to learn of the resurrection message sent especially to Peter by name – "*and Peter*" (Mark 16:7). I feel sure Peter and Mark must have talked it over many a time. What could have more deeply established for Peter the forgiving mercy of the Master, Jesus? It was such a personal and supportive message that in turn John enlarged upon.

"Jesus shewed Himself again to the disciples at the sea of Tiberias; and on this wise shewed He Himself. There were together Simon Peter, and Thomas called Didymus, and Nathanael of Cana in Galilee, and the sons of Zebedee, and two other of His disciples.

"Simon Peter saith unto them, I go a fishing. They say unto him, We also go with thee. They went forth, and entered into a ship immediately; and that night they caught nothing.

"But when the morning was come, Jesus stood on the shore: but the disciples knew not that it was Jesus.

"Then Jesus saith unto them, Children, have ye any meat? They answered Him, No. And He said unto them, Cast the net on the right side of the ship, and ye shall find. They cast therefore, and now they were not able to draw it for the multitudes of fishes.

"Therefore that disciple whom Jesus loved saith unto Peter, It is the Lord. Now when Simon Peter heard that it was the Lord, he girt his fisher's coat unto him (for he was naked), and did cast himself into the sea. And the other disciples came in a little ship; (for they were not far from land, but as it were two hundred cubits,) dragging the net with fishes.

"As soon as they were come to land, they saw a fire of coals there, and fish laid thereon, and bread . . . This is now the third time that Jesus shewed Himself to His disciples, after that He was risen from the dead.

"So when they had dined, Jesus saith to Simon Peter, Simon, son of Jonas, lovest thou Me more than these? He saith unto Him, Yea, Lord; Thou knowest that I love Thee. He saith unto him, Feed My lambs.

"He saith to him again the second time, Simon, son of Jonas, lovest thou Me? He saith unto Him, Yea, Lord; Thou knowest that I love Thee. He saith unto him, Feed My sheep.

"He saith unto him the third time, Simon, son of Jonas, lovest thou Me? Peter was grieved because He said unto him the third time, Lovest thou Me? And he said unto Him, Lord, Thou knowest all things; Thou knowest that I love Thee. Jesus saith unto him, Feed My sheep.

"Verily, verily, I say unto thee, When thou wast young, thou girdedst thyself, and walkedst whither thou wouldest: but when thou shalt be old, thou shalt stretch forth thy hands, and another shall gird thee, and carry thee whither thou wouldest not. This spake He, signifying by what death he should glorify God. And when He had spoken this, He saith unto him, Follow Me.

"Then Peter, turning about, seeth the disciple whom Jesus loved following; which also leaned on His breast at supper, and said, Lord, which is he that betrayeth Thee?

"Peter seeing him saith to Jesus, Lord, and what shall this man do? Jesus saith unto him, If I will that he tarry till I come, what is that to thee? follow thou Me . . . And there are also many other things which Jesus did, the which, if they should be written every one, I suppose that even the world itself could not contain the books that should be written. Amen" (John 21:1-9, 14-22, 25).

*   *   *

Did Mark, I wonder, doubt his youthful right to tell of some of those very personal things in detail?

Angels Everywhere!

I am at a loss now to remember when first I made my acquaintance with angels. It must have been one Christmas, when a more than usually generous number of cards came through the letterbox, with a goodly number of them bearing angels. We always sang the Christmas hymns, of course, and at church the preacher was in the habit of reading of the shepherds in the fields, surprised by heavenly song. But a whole year could go by without our meeting with the angels again. Ours was that kind of home.

The home of the English author of many gentle stories and books widely read, Elizabeth Goudge, was very different. In an article, that I came across, she began by saying: "I was born in 1900, at Wells, in Somersetshire, the cathedral town which I have described . . . in my novel, *A City of Bells* . . . My father was Vice-Principal of the Theological College, and we lived in the house with the tower in which Grandmother Fordyce lived in the book.

"When I was three years old my father became the Principal of the College and we moved across the road to another old house, with carved angels in the corners of the rooms, and there were corners and passages that were wonderful for hide-and-seek.

[It is not therefore surprising that she was early at ease with angels, being moved, years later, to give them a place in her anthology *A Book of Comfort*, that a grown-up Christmas placed on my own shelves.]

"While still revelling in early Christmases, I remember there was one when our full congregation sang:

144

> O hush the noise, ye men of strife,
> And hear the angels sing.

"I didn't properly understand – but I 'hushed'. Still, to my disappointment, I didn't hear the angels sing. It was very puzzling."

Did Mark, in the house where he grew up, do better, I wonder? Of course, when he came to write his little gospel, for some author's reason that I still don't understand, he had no opportunity to tell of the angels on the world's first Christmas, as he started his story when Jesus was grown up. After speaking of John the Baptist, His forerunner, "clothed with camel's hair" (which I always felt would be very prickly), and with a girdle of skin about his loins, there was his voice calling in the wilderness – but no angels' songs! In time, Mark tells of Jesus' forty days in that wild place (Mark 1:12, 13). "And immediately the Spirit driveth Him . . . and He was there . . . forty days, tempted of Satan . . . with the wild beasts; and the angels ministered unto Him." (Not singing this time – here Mark shows us angels doing something else, "ministering".) And it was a long time before I knew what that meant!

Our Lord must have told of that experience Himself, so that it was passed on to Mark by Peter, because there was no one else there with Him at the time. It was right at the beginning of His public ministry. Before the birth of John, it was said, the news that he would be born was brought to his aged father, Zacharias, *by an angel*. It seems that angels often were the bearers of messages in those times – but it was not the messenger but the content of the message itself that left old Zacharias wondering!

Much the same was true of the village maiden Mary, when she was made aware of her role in the Divine pattern of the world's Salvation. And later, when the "given" new life was in the care of Joseph and Mary, and in danger, we read: "An angel appeared to Joseph, by night in a dream, saying: Arise, and take the Young Child and His mother, and flee into Egypt, and be thou there until I bring thee word!" Eventually the word came, telling of vicious Herod's death, and confirming that it was time to return.

On yet another crisis occasion, as Jesus approached the close of His earth-life, we read of His being within the Garden of Gethsemane at His prayer time, which led on to his arrest. A sword was raised in His defence by one of His companions, but the wielder of it was ordered at once to put it back into its place. And Jesus Himself was heard to say: "Thinkest thou that I cannot now pray to my Father, and He shall presently give Me more than twelve legions of angels?"

And again and again, in the early days of the Church that he left on earth to carry His message and ministry, one reads of angels. For those were the days when Christ's followers were always getting into trouble. In the Book of Acts we learn of a number of them "being cast into the common prison". But that, fortunately, was not the end. For we then read: "The angel of the Lord by night opened the prison doors, and brought them forth, and said, Go, stand and speak in the Temple to the people all the words of this life. And when they heard that, they entered into the Temple early in the morning, and taught" (Acts 5:19-21). Of yet another occasion the record says: "And the angel of the Lord spake unto Philip, saying, Arise, and go toward the south . . . And he arose and went" (Acts 8:26-27).

"And . . . the angel of the Lord", we read a little later, "smote Herod, because he gave not God the glory" (Acts 12:23).

So the word "ministry" has a surprisingly wide connotation when applied to angels, as Mark recorded in his very first chapter, summing up Jesus' testing in the Wilderness (Mark 1:13).

And yet, a little further into his writing – in what comes to us as the eighth chapter of Mark's Gospel – he is still accepting as important his Lord's words: "Whomsoever therefore shall be ashamed of Me and of My words in this adulterous and sinful generation; of him also shall the Son of Man be ashamed, when He cometh in the glory of His Father with the holy angels" (8:38).

In his very first chapter, and in his very last (16:5-8), when his book finishes with the glorious loyalty of the women who followed Jesus – bringing their offering of sweet spices, though they were no longer needed on that glorious Resurrection morning – Mark, of set purpose, refers to angels in attendance.

*   *   *

For so, I believe, we are encouraged to interpret Mark's words: "And entering into the sepulchre, they saw a young man sitting on the right side, clothed in a long white garment; and they were affrighted. And he saith unto them, Be not affrighted: Ye seek Jesus of Nazareth, which was crucified: He is risen; He is not here: behold the place where they laid Him" (Mark 16:5-6).

That "long white garment" seems to bother many of us, both young and old. I served in our church bookshop for a number of years, when the war rendered my travelling task impossible, and I shall always remember the day when the Manager looked up from a pile of Christmas mail orders before him, and asked me : "Now think, and tell me if we have anywhere in stock, 'an angel in trousers'? " I replied: "Are there any?" With a smile, Mr Hemer then handed over to me the order which had come from the superintendent of a country Sunday School, who wished to give cards to each of her little flock at Christmas. "But I have one little boy", she wrote, "who doesn't want an angel in a nighty."

I must confess, that even then, a responsible adult a long way from my Sunday school days, I still felt a little confused about angels, and thus full of sympathy for the small boy bespeaking a different kind of card for his Christmas. I reached up, when I returned home that night, and took down an old theological textbook: *What a Christian Believes and Why*, by Dr C.F. Hunter, then in its fourth edition. It had taught me a good deal in my Deaconess training, but it had nothing worthwhile to tell about angels. This was, I suspect, for the simple reason that the learned doctor had not clearly made up his own mind, about what he was obliged to refer to as "the existence of spiritual beings intermediate between God and man", to use his own impressive words. So he neatly slid out of his uncertainty, by quoting someone else, who could only refer to "beings higher than Man, through whom God executes His will, and through whom He ministers to and cares for Man".

But that doesn't, I feel sorry to confess, take us very far. Some angels, of course, are represented as beautiful to behold. I have seen many, as I've journeyed through England's historic and gracious countryside, parish by parish, in homely churches, and in great abbeys and cathedrals. I shall always remember the Spring day when I found my way to Tewkesbury Abbey, rising into the sky with its glorious Norman towers dating back to 1330, and its magnificent lierne vaulting.

Within, I discovered a skilfully set strip of mirror at my feet as I entered the nave, making it possible for me to see clearly the central row of bosses in the high roof over my head. There I saw numerous carved angels – though I was surprised to see some playing a medley of instruments, including a hurdy-gurdy and the bagpipes! I must confess that such a sight seemed to me almost as incongruous as "an angel in trousers".

So my mind is still a little muddled about angels. But the Reverend W.H. Hudspeth, of the British and Foreign Bible Society, working in China, tells us how "an angel appeared unto him, ministering to his need", in the war days, when he lay imprisoned by the Japanese. "One night about eleven," said he, "I was led out by two guards and taken to a room, and given a curt order. On crossing the threshold, wondering what would happen to me, a Japanese, dressed in European clothes, jumped up, and grasping hold of my hand, said: 'I am a Christian, and ever since you were arrested, my wife and I have been praying for you. I cannot get you out of here . . . but I can assure you that you will not be manhandled again.' At that moment, the interrogating officer came in, and though I was questioned until six o'clock the following morning, I was never tortured again. Now, to me," finished Mr Hudspeth, "that Japanese Christian was the Divine hand; he was the modern angel of the Lord!"

Not For a Lie Nor a Legend!

Now that we are within sight of the sudden close of Mark's little gospel, I can never hold the feeling that it is in any way remote, even though it is the earliest of the three that make up "the Synoptic Gospels". Even that once strange Greek word now draws close in its meaning of "to see together". With eagerness I shall go through it again and again, setting out from Mark's first words: "The beginning of the Gospel of Jesus Christ, the Son of God."

And I shall never forget my debt of crispness and closeness of human quality, due to honest Peter's reporting of events outside Mark's personal experience.

For all that, Mark had his own style, even his handful of favourite words that recur, to be welcomed as familiar friends. And how lively they are – wasting no least moment, for all that their message must come to us through translation!

Thanks to Mark's kindly sharing, under unfamiliar skies, we have travelled far; and shared with our Master's first disciples, some of His closest teaching. And we have known appreciation of simple, beautiful things of the every day, as a new delight. We have made friends in home and marketplace, even to one early morning – never to be forgotten – when a little handful of faithful women came to their loved Master's tomb, bearing sweet spices. At first, our combined strengths left us, as we knew that we could never move the mighty stone over the doorway of His sepulchre.

Then, of a sudden – thanks to Mark's words – we found ourselves sharing this world's greatest wonder with those faithful souls bearing sweet spices that were to remain unused – for Death has been conquered. And our Lord is risen! The stone is rolled away! A young man in white speaks!

Mark reports this, in his very last chapter! "Be not affrightened!" he sets down as the words of the young heaven-sent messenger. "Ye seek Jesus of Nazareth, which was crucified: He is risen; He is not here: behold the place where they laid Him. But go your way, tell His disciples and Peter that He goeth before you into Galilee: there shall ye see Him, as He said unto you. And they went out quickly, and fled from the sepulchre; for they trembled and were amazed: neither said they any thing to any man; for they were afraid . . ." (Mark 16:6-8).

And at this point, Mark's words as recorded in his recognizable style, suddenly cease. Learned scholars, saints, and ordinary disciples like ourselves have spent long hours examining the verses that remain, more than half the final verses that now round off the story.

One of our modern scholars, commenting in *The Interpreter's Bible*, asks: "Was the final page of Mark's gospel lost? Perhaps he never finished the story."

"Vocabulary, style and content", says yet another commentator, "are unquestionably non-Marcan, and have a distinct flavour of the second century."

"We have only to read the passage to see how different it is from the rest of the gospels," says Dr William Barclay, "and it is in none of the great manuscripts of the gospels. This is a later summary which replaces the ending which either Mark did not live to write, or which at some time was lost.

"Its great interest", he adds, "is the picture of the duty of the Church that it gives to us. The man who wrote the concluding section obviously believed that the Church had certain tasks committed to it by Jesus."

*   *   *

During the time that I have been specially studying Mark's gift to the world, besides Dr Barclay, another close Christian writer has died: Dr E M Blaiklock, Professor of Classics at Auckland University. He lived just across the valley from our tree-blessed garden and home at "West Hills", for the whole of the sixteen years that Rene and I lived high uplifted there. He and I, both busy writers, did not see much of each other – though we could look across and see each other's study windows, and know that behind them was being written another book to go out into the world. He wrote a great many, some of which earned him world recognition. He also travelled a great deal and broadcast constantly – so that we had many interests in common when we met before his glowing fire of logs, or he with his wife, before ours. And few evenings together there were, in one place or the other, when the talk was not of Palestine, or Greece, and, of course, of books! Rene was a vital Presbyterian; the doctor and his loved wife, devoted Baptists; and myself a trained Deaconess of the Methodist Church. I don't think we ever talked denominationally – though the doctor and I listened to each others' lectures occasionally, and much oftener to each others' broadcasts. From time to time we exchanged books, and talked of their reception.

Some of his books were learned, and handsomely bound by classical world presses; some but paperback study books. One such that he gave me lies before me at this moment, entitled *The Young Man Mark*, a companion study with that of my other friend, Dr William Barclay's study paperback, *The Gospel of Mark*.

"Christ rose from the dead. That fact above all others", wrote my learned friend from across the valley, "makes the Gospel of Mark a real and living story! Mark drew much of it from Peter, so ancient tradition tells us . . . the Peter who looked up into the empty tomb, and talked with the Risen Christ on the beach in the dawn. So sure was Peter", adds my friend, "that he died for his faith in Rome about the time Mark wrote his gospel. He was crucified head downwards. Men do not face a ghastly death like that for 'a lie or a legend'. And Mark himself died not long afterwards. We think he was then in Rome . . . and it was a dangerous time to be there, with Nero's last mad days decimating the Church. The gospel certainly seems to have been finished in haste. (See chapter 16:8. Mark's style breaks off at that point – proof of another hand.) It could, of course, be that Mark had chosen to end it there – but that is not very likely. It could be that there was the clash of grounded spearbutts in some Roman courtyard; or a harsh battering on the door, and the hasty thrusting of hurried last pages into concealment – and the end . . . ''

*   *   *

O Lord of Life, Thy quickening voice,
Awakes my morning song!
In gladsome words I would rejoice
That I to Thee belong.

I see Thy light, I feel Thy wind;
The world it is Thy word;
Whatever wakes my heart and mind,
Thy presence is, my Lord.

Therefore I choose my highest part,
And turn my face to Thee,
Therefore I stir my inmost heart
To worship fervently.

Lord, let me live and will this day,
Keep rising from the dead;
Lord, make my spirit good, and gay –
Give me my daily bread.

Within my heart speak, Lord, speak on,
My heart alive to keep.
Till comes the night, and labour done;
In Thee I fall asleep.

George MacDonald,
sensitive Christian poet

I REJOICE IN MARK'S
LIVING, LASTING GOSPEL!

Acknowledgements

The author and publisher are grateful for permission to use the following extracts in this book:

An extract on page 81 taken from a talk by Bryan Paynter, used with his permission and that of the New Zealand Broadcasting Corporation. An extract from *No Uncertain Sound* by Leonard Small, published by T. and T. Clark, Edinburgh, 1963. An extract from *Christ and His Cross* by W.R. Maltby, published by Epworth Press.

Quotations from the works of Dr William Barclay, Dr J.S. Stewart, Gilbert Thomas and Dr E.M. Blaiklock throughout the book are used with the authors' personal permission.

Unless otherwise stated, quotations from the Bible are taken from the Authorized Version.

Also available in Fount Paperbacks

BOOKS BY RITA SNOWDEN

Discoveries That Delight

'Thirty brief chapters of reflections on selected psalms . . . The book is very readable. Its style has been achieved through many years of work to produce a vehicle of religious communication with a wide appeal.'

Neville Ward, Church of England Newspaper

Further Good News

'Another enjoyable book from Rita Snowden; easy to read and with a store of good things to ponder over and store in the mind. The author shows clearly that there is much Good News in our world and that this is very much the gift of a loving God.'

Church Army Review

I Believe Here and Now

'Once again she has produced for us one of the most readable and helpful pieces of Christian witness I have seen . . .'

D. P. Munro, Life and Work

A Woman's Book of Prayer

'This book will make prayer more real and meaningful for all who use it. There is all through the book an accent of reality. Here the needs of the twentieth century are brought to God in twentieth century language.'

William Barclay

More Prayers for Women

'. . . she has that rare and valuable gift of being able to compose forms of prayer which really do express the aspirations of many people . . .'

Philip Cecil, Church Times

Fount Paperbacks

Fount is one of the leading paperback publishers of religious books and below are some of its recent titles.

- [ ] THE WAY OF THE CROSS Richard Holloway £1.95
- [ ] LIKE WIND ON THE GRASSES Rita Snowden £1.95
- [ ] AN INTRODUCTION TO MARITAL PROBLEMS Jack Dominian £2.50
- [ ] I AM WITH YOU John Woolley £2.95
- [ ] NOW AND FOR EVER Anne Townsend £1.95
- [ ] THE PERFECTION OF LOVE Tony Castle £2.95
- [ ] A PROPHETIC PEOPLE Clifford Hill £2.95
- [ ] THOMAS MORE Richard Marius £7.95
- [ ] WALKING IN THE LIGHT David Winter £1.95
- [ ] HALF WAY Jim Thompson £2.50
- [ ] THE HEART OF THE BIBLE George Appleton £4.95
- [ ] I BELIEVE Trevor Huddleston £1.75
- [ ] PRESENT CONCERNS C. S. Lewis £1.95
- [ ] PSALMS OF PRAISE Frances Hogan £2.50
- [ ] MOTHER TERESA: CONTEMPLATIVE IN THE HEART OF THE WORLD Angelo Devananda £2.50
- [ ] IN THE HURRICANE Adrian Hastings £2.50

All Fount paperbacks are available at your bookshop or newsagent, or they can be ordered by post from Fount Paperbacks, Cash Sales Department, G.P.O. Box 29, Douglas, Isle of Man, British Isles. Please send purchase price plus 15p per book, maximum postage £3. Customers outside the UK send purchase price, plus 15p per book. Cheque, postal order or money order. No currency.

NAME (Block letters)_____

ADDRESS_____

_____